Every Family is Special

LOVE COMES FIRST

Jan Blaustone

DEACONESS PRESS
Minneapolis

Library of Congress Cataloging-in-Publication Data

Blaustone, Jan.

    Every family is special : love comes first / by Jan Blaustone.

      p.   cm.

    ISBN 0-925190-72-1

    1. Family—United States—Case studies.   2. Family life surveys—

United States.   I. Title.

HQ536.B538   1994

306.85'0973—dc20   94-9564

                                               CIP

Partial proceeds of the sale of this book will be donated to The National Committee to Prevent Child Abuse and their national program, Healthy Families America.

Published by Deaconess Press (a service of Riverside Medical Center, a division of Fairview Hospital and Healthcare Services, 2450 Riverside Avenue South, Minneapolis, MN 55454).

Cover and interior page design by The Nancekivell Group.

In Chapter One, all songs by Lisa Silver/Wendy Spira, Sweet Silver Music/Han Harry Music © 1991, Nashville, TN. Page 11 quote © 1993 by Libby Leverett Crew. "My Wish for You," page 21 © 1992 by Cheryl Hutton.

First Printing: April 1994.

Printed in the United States of America.

97 96 95 94   7 6 5 4 3 2 1

Publisher's Note: Deaconess Press publishes books and other materials related to the subjects of physical health, mental health, and chemical dependency. Its publications, including *Every Family is Special,* do not necessarily reflect the philosophy of Fairview Hospital and Healthcare Services or their treatment programs.

For a current catalog of Deaconess Press titles, please call this Toll-Free number: 1–800–544–8207.

*This book is lovingly
dedicated to the family,
yours and mine.*

Acknowledgments

There are many people who helped make this book possible. I would like to thank a few of them now because I can never thank them enough.

Thank you to my "first" family for starting me out on the right path: Thanks, Mom. You'll always be my biggest hero. Thanks, Gary, my big, big brother. Mom wrote in my baby book that you cried after she scolded me once when I was eighteen months old. It was obvious even then that your heart was huge. Now it's so big, there's no way you can hide it. And thanks, Dad. I know you're still watching, and I hope that you're smiling.

Thank you to my "second" family, Michael and Lee, for putting up with five-foot-tall piles of laundry, dirty dishes, and eating pasta for months straight while I chased my dreams into the night. A part of you is on every page: Thanks, Sweetie. It's your turn now. Thanks, my little pumpkin. If the fish aren't biting, let's go to the park!

Thank you, Jay and Ed, for your confidence and for the opportunity to share encouraging words with others. Lastly, a special thanks to all fifteen families profiled in this book. They endured many lengthy late-night conversations, endless personal questions, and interruptions into their own familytime. And when I enlisted their help again in critiquing their stories, they didn't even whimper. Thanks to everyone for your patience, but most of all, thank you for your humbling honesty and inspiration.

PHOTOGRAPHS

I gratefully acknowledge the spectacular contributions from photographers who helped make this book special. All photographs are copyrighted and they are used with permission. Please note that not all the photographs used in this book depict actual subjects from the family profiles. Those photographs which show actual family members from the profiles are indicated below, and most of these were taken by actual family or friends of the subjects in my interviews.

Front cover hand-tinted photograph by Gail Goodwin, entitled "By the Seashore." Photographs p. viii by Libby Leverett Crew (subjects are Larry Crew and little Allison Crew from the Chapter 1 profile); p. 10 by Libby Leverett Crew (hands are of Allison Crew and her grandfather, Les Leverett); p. 44, 52 by Libby Leverett Crew; p. xiv, 20, 104, 114, 150, 160 by Mary Entrekin; p. 32, 124 by Pam Demonbreun; p. 60 by Nancy Libby (subject is Evan Libby); p. 72, 162 by Ross Smith; p. 82 by Linda Thompson Chandler (subjects are Gary Chandler and son, Alex); p. 94 by Michelle Fielden (subjects are Louise Stark and her mother, Anne); p. 136 by Walt Null (subjects are Lynn and Dan Kirkbride and their five children, taken on their ranch: bottom row, left to right, Jeremy, Charlie, Lynn, Mick; top row, left to right, Hannah, Dan, and Abby); and p. 164 by Dave Marion (subjects are Jan and Michael Blaustone and their son, Lee).

TABLE OF CONTENTS

INTRODUCTION

This is a book about fifteen families who opened their hearts to a stranger. Over the course of several months, I asked them questions ranging from religion to relationships, questions about their biggest regrets, their biggest triumphs, and their highest of hopes. They answered me with the entire family listening in on the other line, and again later, all alone. I wrote their stories taking the same direction of our many conversations together. Some went left and some went right. Sometimes they didn't like what I wrote, and sometimes they were embarrassed. After much consideration and many revisions, they all agreed to share their stories with you. And in the end, they all were proud of what they had to share.

Every family in this book is unique. They aren't famous outside their own families but they are all real people, although some have chosen to use fictitious names. During the last year I talked with countless parents whom I found inspiring. Some were introduced to me through friends, some have been long-time family friends, and others were mere business acquaintances. Regardless of whether I knew these families previously, now it feels that I've known them forever.

Many readers have asked me why I selected these particular fifteen families. It's because every time we spoke I got goosebumps, and sometimes, a giant lump in my throat. These are the people who moved me the most. Their stories are not only inspiring, they are unforgettable. Join me in celebrating each family's uniqueness, their courage, their faith, and their powerful love of life. These are everyday people living everyday lives in extraordinary ways. I'll never forget them. After reading their stories, I doubt you will ever forget them either.

Some of the families are single parents by choice while others did not choose to be single, but are. Some are immigrant families who began life with "nothing" and now have "everything." And there are those who began life with "everything" and now have "nothing." You will meet mothers who left their careers at forty and others who began their careers at eighty. There are grandparents who teach family heritage and young mothers who chose to teach at home. There are parents who learn from their disabled children and parents with disabilities who give the lessons of their life to us all. You'll find sons burdened with regret and the fathers who loved them. There are fathers who share their passions with their sons. And there are daughters who care passionately for their aging mothers. There are parents with second chances who begin life again alongside the children who inspire them. And you'll meet those who have run out of second chances altogether.

One father will tell you, "Mirrors aren't real friendly." He was, perhaps, the most honest interviewee of all, although he didn't always like what he saw in his mirror. If I were to line everyone up in front of that mirror, you would see people spanning the ages, from babies to ninety-year-olds. Some are white, some black, some short, some tall, and there are many, many different people in between.

In spite of their differences, the one thing every family has in common, the one attribute none can live without, is *love*. Love is their common denominator. The parents profiled in this book all love life, they love living, and they love sharing it with their children. They acknowledge their hardships, their regrets, and their fears. And they give praise for their blessings. They love their families. They love their roots. They simply *love*. These parents put their families first, no matter what the odds, and no matter what the sacrifices. They all want what is best for their children, and they will go to great lengths to give their children opportunities that they never had. They are resilient and courageous. Some are generations apart and yet, they are the same. They are a small, but powerful reflection of America's family, past and present.

Every family is special. Every family has a story to tell. I have a story, and so do you. My family is Caucasian, German, Cambodian and Chinese—and there are only three of us! Other families profiled here are African American, Native American, and Latino. Some parents are white and their children are black. Some families have adopted, while others have not. Some, like myself, are the daughters of blue-collar workers, while other parents are farmers, police officers, cotton-pickers, photographers, doctors, musicians, and politicians. I sometimes need to use a wheelchair, and think of it as a nuisance. Others, as you will see, feel their wheelchairs signify freedom. Our son is not disabled or mentally challenged, but other children you will meet are different than he. I am almost forty years old, while others here are more than twice my age. And yet, some are only four years old.

We all have something to say about our families, and if I were to live 100 years, it still wouldn't be long enough to document the diverse heroics of family life. Here are fifteen different stories about fifteen different families who, in their own way, will tell you the same thing: LOVE COMES FIRST.

Motherhood
is a proud profession
never intended for cowards.

Chapter One

HOLDING ON TO THE DREAM

Dreams, like people, come in different shapes and sizes. Lisa Silver had already fulfilled one of her dreams by age forty. She's in steady demand as a musician, background singer, and songwriter. To succeed in the music industry is a challenging goal in a fickle business. You must love the craft for your own pleasure before you can achieve any degree of success. It takes years of dedication and perseverance to make even a modest living at it. Lisa is good at her craft because she loves her work and has been tenacious about achieving her level of success. It is with the same passion and tenacity that she chased her second dream in life—being a mom.

"I was never really 'attached' to the idea of marriage or giving birth. What I longed for was a child, someone to love and nurture and watch grow. What was missing in my life was motherhood." But how does a single woman go about fulfilling her dream of motherhood?

"You have to do what you think is right. For me, adoption was the right choice." After months of research and networking, Lisa learned that the right choice for her was next to impossible. Door after door was closed to the very idea of a single person wanting to adopt. Even Lisa's closest friends and family questioned her dream of becoming a single parent by choice.

" 'What if this happens, what if that happens …,' they kept saying. 'Do you really know what you're getting into? What if your baby's not healthy? Have you lost your mind? You're thirty-eight years old and single—enjoy it!' "

The more people told Lisa she was crazy for wanting to be a single parent, the more Lisa knew she was right. Rather than believing what everyone told her, Lisa became increasingly confident that she *would* make a good single parent. And how does anyone ever really know whether their baby will be healthy? Lisa was determined to keep looking for that open door.

"I can do this," she kept thinking. "It *is* possible. Sure it's risky, but what isn't? I have a lot of love to share and somewhere out there is a little person who's in need of my love and attention. I just have to keep looking."

After several years of exploring adoption channels, Lisa's dreams of music and motherhood crossed paths. During a recording session, Lisa ran into an old acquaintance from Detroit named Wendy Spira. Wendy was a single woman who had recently adopted a baby girl from India. Wendy instantly became Lisa's closest mentor, and she told her about a support group in Chicago formed exclusively for single adoptive parents. The group was made up of single men and women wading through "red tape" during the adoption process and also many who had already successfully adopted.

Lisa arranged her Nashville work schedule so that she could attend the next support group meeting in Chicago. While there, she met a variety of hopeful single people like herself and, in particular, the families of single women who had adopted children from other countries. "I always knew it was possible, but meeting those women and children encouraged me more than ever." During her stay in Chicago that weekend, Lisa met a little boy named Luis who melted her heart like no other child had.

"I'd been considering an international adoption, but I wasn't sure if it was right for me until I met Luis, who was born in South America. He stole my heart away. After that, I was convinced that a Bolivian-born child could be the answer to my dream. I left Chicago with new strength and assurance. Not only was I certain that single parenthood was right for me, now I knew that my baby was out there, and I also knew where—in Bolivia!"

Lisa's following months became a roller coaster ride of uncertainty and chaos. The paperwork involved in a Bolivian adoption was harder than Lisa ever imagined. Rules were changed in midstream. There were official stamps, seals, and signatures required. Lisa needed her home study updated and reprocessed with the State Department of Human Services. She was fingerprinted and waded through numerous immigration and visa requirements. She kept filing additional medical forms, all the while contending with the language barriers. There were consulate appointments, lawyers, and then even more lawyers. Schedules were constantly changing and she missed several international flights … Lisa's dream was turning into a nightmare!

Throughout the entire process was the waiting, waiting, waiting. To help her cope, Lisa turned her attention to her craft. Her frustrations became journal entries that began rhyming and taking on meter. In a short while, a collection of songs was born. Lisa's lyrics spoke of real life emotions, passion, empathy, and hope. Next, Lisa collaborated over the course of a year with her mentor and talented friend, Wendy, to co-write and produce an entire album celebrating adoptive families.

Their 1991 record, entitled *My Forever Family*, was inspired by Wendy and Lisa's dreams of motherhood and by unique, colorful children like Wendy's four-year-old daughter. Their passionate love for children translated into a gift of music that could be shared by many. International adoptions had a special place in their hearts, as celebrated in the verse of one song ….

> *I've got two countries, two countries*
> *To call my very own*
> *The country I was born in*
> *And the country I call home.*

Finally, some fourteen months after her adoption process began, Lisa's long-awaited day in South America arrived. On August 9, 1991, five-month-old Olivia Juliana was placed tenderly in her new mother's arms. Lisa knew, in an instant, the joy that Wendy had spoken of. She also knew that her entire adoption ordeal was well worth the struggle and frustration.

"Olivia smiled when she looked at me! She was so tiny and adorable, with lots of black hair and big black eyes. I was instantly in love. Now, when I flash back on all those days of frustration during the adoption process, they're insignificant—just a little blip in time!"

Lisa realized both her dreams in life, music *and* motherhood, and they've complimented each other. "Since adopting Olivia, my perspective about the music I write has changed. I wrote country music for the last twenty years, and now I'm seeing Latin influences in some of my writing. Olivia has not only taught me about motherhood, she's brought me the gift of a whole culture I previously knew nothing about. Bolivia is a fascinating place, and it's a thrill for me to share her own culture with others through my music. It's a wonderful sound."

Almost three years later, Lisa can't picture what her life would be without Olivia. Single parenting *is* a challenge, but for Lisa, it's also her biggest dream come true.

"I can't imagine feeling any more bonded to a child if I'd given birth myself. When I look at Olivia, I see my own expressions and I hear my own phrasing and voice inflections. We're a part of each other. She's two and a half now, and still so beautiful that she takes my breath away. The only real surprise is that Olivia is the organized one and I'm still spilling my milk. I'm only just now becoming confident as a parent. Maybe I'm doing okay after all.

"While I'm grateful for my success in the music industry, I know that my daughter's adoption was nothing less than a miracle for me. I've been truly blessed. Olivia and I have our ups and downs, just like in the music business, but my work is no longer the most important aspect in my life. The scales may tip a little, back and forth, but now there is a balance.

"I chose two directions in my life and neither had an easy route. I've heard a lot of doors shut. Friends kept reminding me how difficult parenting was, and that I was nuts to want to go it alone. Single parenting isn't right for everyone. But now more than ever, I know that it's right for me—me and Olivia, that is."

Towering over me
My little child
Was it not so long ago
When you were small
And I was large
And your little hand
I would hold?

— Libby Leverett Crew

Chapter Two

CRAZY IN LOVE

It was one of those fall days when the breeze blows gently by for as long as you sit on the porch swing. After our long hot summer, everyone welcomed this cool, dry breeze. Libby, her husband, Larry, and I sipped iced tea on their back porch and we talked in lazy tones, not caring where the conversation would lead.

Libby described her parents with such pride that you might have thought she was talking about her own children. "After forty-six years of marriage and the death of three babies, Momma and Daddy still hold hands," she boasted. "They say their marriage just keeps getting better. Daddy toasted in their fortieth anniversary by telling Momma, 'Come grow old with me; the best is yet to be.' Now, that's the way it should be."

Libby spoke with a slow and husky Southern drawl. She chose her words carefully, as if they fell short when describing her parents. Even a stranger could see that Libby knew she was loved by her parents, as much as any daughter could.

"Ten years ago on my wedding day, I told Momma that I fell in love with my husband the first time I laid eyes on him. Momma told me that she remembered the night I introduced Larry to her, and she also fell in love with him. She said her love was because of the moon and that wonderful things can happen during full moons because that's when I was born. Then she told me that she never thought she could love anyone as much as she loved my daddy—at least not until she laid eyes on an 'angel' born thirty-four years ago during a full moon. I remember thinking I was anything but an angel while I hugged Momma, letting her enjoy the moment."

Libby looked down at the sleeping baby girl in her arms, and then she looked back at me. "I didn't know how much my parents really loved me until I held our daughter, Allison. Then I knew in an instant." Her blue eyes were filled with tears and she said, "How did they ever let me go?"

Margaret Allison Crew was also born on the eve of a full moon. Twenty-two days later, her young birth mother placed her lovingly into Libby's arms.

Little baby Allison doesn't look like her new adoptive parents because Allison is biracial and Larry and Libby are not. Libby says that she, too, has mixed races in her own heritage, but not African American, like Allison. Yet, in a peculiar sort of way, Allie has Larry's dark curly hair and Libby's big dimples when she smiles. "There's nothing like a baby's toothless grin. Allie can make even the grumpiest man smile," Libby said. And she's right—I've seen this baby turn on the charm. Every time Allison smiled at me, I forgot what I was thinking.

Libby's also right when she says that she and Allison, like all of us, are the same color on the inside. "Absolute strangers will come up and carry on lengthy conversations with me when they see Allison. People of all races and all ages carry on like we're family. When I take her for her morning stroll, the neighbors actually come running out of their houses to visit. Some of our neighbors we've hardly spoken to, until we adopted Allie. Little Jaime, who's eight and lives down the street, is a biracial girl with a white brother and sister. When I stroll by the park, Jaime comes running over with her friends saying, 'Oh, she's so pretty! She's just like me!' "

For Larry and Libby, their life was profoundly changed when Allison became part of their family. Libby had previously miscarried her only pregnancy. She felt a loss like any mother feels when her child dies. "But I believe one's soul is separate from the body," said Libby, "and that our only child's soul is alive in our new baby daughter, Allison. Holding Allie is as natural to us as it would be for any parent holding their only living child. Once we finally became parents, we never wanted to let our daughter out of our sight. Even when Allie had colic, we didn't want to be away from her!"

"Life changes so quickly," added Larry, "you should never lose hope. Libby and I were in our most depressed state ever just two hours before Allison's birth mother called and decided to entrust her daughter's life with us. We had just about given up. Libby had sat on this very porch drinking wine and blowing soap bubbles until her jaw hurt. Then she got up and went for a walk. When she returned, we got the call. Two days later, we were parents. You can wait forever, but when lightning strikes, it strikes hard."

"Now I don't know whether to invest in Pampers or Kleenex," said Libby.

Momma Libby writes a letter to Allison every month on the 26th, the anniversary of their parenthood. Then she neatly tapes it into Allie's baby book. "Someday I hope Allison will open her baby book and realize just how much she means to us. We really didn't know how big the void was until Allison came into our life and filled it."

I remember that special day, too. My husband and I were the first stop Larry and Libby made while returning home with their new baby daughter. Our toddler shrieked the loudest, joining in with us adults. We stood around for an hour in disbelief, staring and slobbering all over Allison. Kleenex was in big demand that morning!

Our son wanted to kiss Allison first, and then he asked her where she had been. It was a simple question that none of us could answer. He held her tiny hand tenderly and stared down at her with two-year-old wonder as we chattered on and on. Then it was my turn to hold her. With both children in my lap, I looked down at Allison's little fingers curled around our son's chubby forefinger. In an instant, I was reminded of how big our boy had grown in his short two, almost three, years of life. His hand looked huge and manlike next to Allie's tiny features. I still thought of him as our little baby boy, my own little pumpkin. I guess mothers always do that, no matter what their child's age. Holding a newborn again, I realized why it is that babies make me cry: Life is too precious not to.

That afternoon, Momma Libby, Daddy Larry and Little Allison left our driveway, and Larry got his very first speeding ticket. Welcome to Parenthood. Libby carefully taped his citation into Allie's Baby Book later that evening.

With a smirk on her face, she said that Larry has also absentmindedly thrown their dirty dishes and silverware into the garbage. Larry countered, saying that in the two months that followed Allison's adoption, Libby more than made up for his mistakes.

Once, while Allison napped, Libby ran frantically around the house doing chores while clinging to a stick of deodorant she mistook for the baby monitor. Then there was the morning she called me up and screamed, "My nipples are burning! My nipples are burning!", and then she slammed down the phone. Confused, I hung up my phone, too. I was *sure* she wasn't breastfeeding. Later that morning, Larry woke up to the lingering smell of burning rubber coming from the kitchen. Libby, meanwhile, had to run to the store to buy new baby bottle nipples. She had left the old ones boiling on the stove too long while we chatted on the phone.

So the parenting journey begins in the household of Larry, Libby, and Allison Crew. Larry and Libby's once-beloved houseplants are dying because neither seems to notice that the greenery needs water to survive. On my way out, I mention to Libby that a big clay pot is tipped over on its side in the living room. She glanced over at the dirt spilled onto their new white carpet and said matter-of-factly, "You know, someone else noticed that, too."

More "seasoned" parents can only smile and advise Larry and Libby to enjoy the ride, for life passes by so quickly. Libby's parents will tell them that wonderful things happen when there is a full moon. But really, none of this needs to be told to these new parents. And Libby doesn't need Allison's Baby Book to let her daughter know that she is loved. All Libby needs to do is remember the love that her parents gave her.

"There's a lot of truth in the saying that you begin learning how to become a good parent during your childhood," said Libby. "The first lesson my parents taught me was how to love unconditionally." It's a special kind of love that is handed down through the generations. Allison's grandmother once told Libby that she never thought she could love anyone as much as she loved her husband. "At least not until she laid eyes on an 'angel' born thirty-four years ago during a full moon." Libby never fully understood her mother's words of love until now.

As I started to leave, Larry and Libby hugged me goodbye. Again, Libby's eyes filled up with tears. She glanced down at baby Allison, asleep in her arms, and in a broken voice she whispered to me, "I still can't believe that I've finally come face to face with an angel of my own."

MY WISH FOR YOU

Let sunshine warm your every day
and light the path you walk
Let laughter be your loudest voice
and truthful be your talk.

Let happiness sustain your heart
and compassion be its beat
Let music be the sounds you hear
and all you hear be sweet.

Let beauty fill your every vision
and honest be your eyes
Let fairness be your judgement guide
and your minds be strong and wise.

Let worthiness assume your soul
and patience be your stand
Let loving ways adorn yourself
Tender be your hands.

All these things I wish for you
and the children that you bear
For qualities like these my loves
are often much too rare.

I wish that I could make them gifts
but they must come from you
You have to work to give them life
in all you say and do.

Chapter Three

BELIEVE IN YOURSELF

Cheryl Anne has always been rebellious. During her adolescence, she was never content to spend a Saturday night at home with her family. Cheryl preferred to be out "running with the wrong crowd" and testing her curfew, along with her parents' patience. She never listened when they advised her to choose friends carefully, especially her boyfriends. Naturally, when Cheryl began a relationship with Kirby, a man seven years older than herself, she defiantly ignored her parents' warnings.

At nineteen years of age, Cheryl married Kirby. On the eve of their honeymoon, her new husband sat her down and told her clearly just "how things are going to be from now on."

"Here I was, this kid who never listened to anyone before, and now I was being told exactly how to live ... or else." Or else what? Kirby made her so afraid of him that she never wanted to find out. "He was very threatening in a suggestive kind of way."

Cheryl's husband made her account for every minute of her time, or he said she would have "hell to pay." He made it clear that he was in charge of her life from that day forward, and she was never to cross him.

"*That* warning I heard loud and clear, and it came from someone I thought I knew. I'd never been so wrong in my life."

For the next nine years, Cheryl lived looking over her shoulder in fear. "Kirby was extremely insecure and jealous. He demanded explanations every time I was five or ten minutes late coming home from work, and then he'd check my alibis!" It was a hideous way to live and Cheryl had no idea how to change it. This man whom Cheryl once thought she knew was now a stranger to her and becoming more obsessive with every passing day.

During their fifth year of marriage, Kirby insisted on her becoming pregnant, saying it would improve their relationship. As usual, she didn't argue and nine months later, Jason was born.

"My husband preferred me being pregnant. While he lightened up during those months, he immediately put the pressure back on for a second child right after I delivered Jason. Then I realized what was happening. Kirby felt that when I was pregnant, he had nothing to worry about because what man would ever be interested in a pregnant woman?" Eighteen months later, their second child, Ashley, was born.

Finally, during their eighth year of marriage, Cheryl and Kirby agreed to see a marriage counselor. The professional guidance she received was anything but consoling. Their counselor advised her in private to "check for any possible weapons in the house, and if you find any guns, leave immediately." Cheryl nervously searched their apartment one afternoon for a weapon and her excuse to leave him.

She found no hidden gun. Kirby's weapon wasn't made of metal. His power over her was created through intimidation and fear. Cheryl's conscience began overshadowing her abusive and volatile eight-year marriage. Finally, for the sake of her children, she felt she had to leave Kirby and the three of them begin a new and peaceful life together.

"Kirby's love for me had developed into an obsession. But I also realized that his paranoia was going to ruin the lives of our children. I could see them slowly becoming his pawns, living a life of fear and anxiety." Cheryl decided to divorce her husband. She gathered up her courage to confront him and played the scene over and over in her mind. Several weeks passed before Cheryl felt the confidence to tell Kirby the news.

"Perhaps he sensed my decision, because the very afternoon I planned to tell him, I returned from work to an empty apartment. He took everything! Jason and Ashley were gone, our bank accounts were drained … he left one month's rent on the kitchen counter, and he completely disappeared. If Kirby had left the kids behind and taken everything else, I would have been grateful. Instead, he took what mattered to me most—the children. I felt devastated, but also more angry than I'd ever been in my whole life."

Cheryl crumbled onto the floor of her empty apartment and cried. Then she turned her anger and devastation into strength and determination. She rose and stood tall for the first time since her honeymoon, and she told herself that she'd never, ever lose control of her life again. She vowed to locate her two children if it was the last thing she ever did. She'd *never* give up looking for them. The rebel inside Cheryl returned that afternoon when her husband left.

"I didn't care what it took. I wanted back in charge of my life, and I wanted my children free from any harm or oppression. I vowed not to stop until I found them, and when I did, to move them to safety and never look back."

Cheryl was lucky. In a matter of days, Kirby contacted her, and he soon returned home with the children. He did not contest their divorce, nor did he seek legal custody of their children. Six months later, the divorce was final and Cheryl received full custody of the children. They never saw Kirby again.

"But more important, I got my life back so I could raise Jason and Ashley the way they deserved. When Kirby and I were divorced, Jason was four and Ashley was three. That was seven years ago and, thankfully, they don't remember much about those days."

Now Cheryl looks back on her life and realizes that her parents were right about her all along. "I was a smart ass, but they've always loved me in spite of it. They knew immediately that I was different from my brother and sisters and that I'd have to learn about life the hard way. I'm sure it broke their hearts to watch me fall in and out of trouble. But they also knew that I was no dummy and that I would eventually wake up.

"Actually, I don't think my parents ever really knew what a dangerous situation I'd gotten myself into with my marriage. It's probably best they didn't know. At least I spared them *that* pain. Every parent wants what's best for their children. My parents did a good job with their children, and I hope I do a good job raising mine, too. When Jason was ten, he started complaining about 'equal rights for kids.' Our conversation went like this:

> 'Fine. If you want equal rights, then you have to share equal responsibilities. Your third of the household expenses is $500 per month. Since you want to set your own bedtime, you need to cough up your share of the expenses.'
>
> 'How do you expect me to do that? I'm just a kid!'
>
> 'Exactly. End of discussion.'

"I think the reason I have two gorgeous children today is so I can survive. *They* are my reason to carry on, and they always have been. They keep me going when times get tough. They're what keeps my feet on the ground. *And* they make me listen. For the first time in my life, I've learned to listen. Of course, they never hesitate to make their opinions known either. But they see things in people that I still don't see. They're intuitive. I think most kids see things that adults are often oblivious to.

"My relationships with men are long-term and very infrequent. It's a game of chance whether I'll ever meet someone we *all* feel good about. I wouldn't remarry just for me or just for my kids. I don't need a man to take care of me. I never want a relationship where my husband solely takes care of me and the kids. Marriage is a partnership, and I want to know that if my husband may drop dead tomorrow, I can still swing things. *Together* we should take care of each other.

"So, If I find someone, fine. If not, that's okay too. But who knows what will happen in life? Anything's possible and I'm still open to possibilities. I'm not in love with single parenting, but I *am* in love with my children. My biggest challenge and concern isn't with finding a spouse, but in finding time to spend with my kids."

It is especially difficult for a single parent to accomodate each child's interests. "Jason is in Boy Scouts, and he also plays ball. So on Tuesdays at 5:00 p.m., I take him to practice. Wednesdays at 5:30 p.m., he has a Scouts meeting. Thursdays from 5–7:00 p.m. are his nights for ball practice—again. Saturday's at 11:00 a.m. is his league's game, and once a month after practice he has a pack meeting. Sometimes it seems that we spend most of our time together riding in the car!"

"Then there's Ashley…. Fortunately, she enjoys watching her brother play ball." Jason's many outside activities allow Cheryl to spend more time with her daughter. Ashley and her mother are extremely close and Cheryl feels there is little, if anything, that her daughter would not talk to her about.

Cheryl feels that the biggest blessing since her divorce is a man named Sean who has become Jason's "Big Buddy." Sean "joined" her family three years ago through her local "Buddies of Nashville" program, affiliated with the national Big Brothers/Big Sisters of America organization. Although Cheryl is incredibly independent and strong, she admits that she could use some help. "Sean is a great male influence for Jason especially. Jason feels he can talk to Sean about things he prefers not to ask me about. And Sean is always there for Jason, either by phone or in person. He's a balance in our family that I couldn't fill."

Considering her marriage to Kirby, Cheryl was reluctant to ever trust a man again. Her standards for a Big Buddy were so high, she really never thought the program could recommend anyone who fit the bill.

"I was extremely demanding. I went above and beyond the usual criteria. I wanted a man not only in my age group with similar beliefs and concerns, but I requested someone who was well educated, too. Sean is from Turkey, he's very intelligent and wise, and he has lived here for twenty years. He has his Ph.D. in engineering, but he remains very simple and practical. Most important, he *loves* the children. Jason couldn't have a better buddy. We all adore Sean. He's indispensable to us."

"Without a doubt, the hardest job I'll ever face in life is being a good parent. While growing up, I was fortunate to have two parents who cared—great people, salt of the earth. They watched as I made a lot of big mistakes in life, but that was how I learned. I'm especially thankful that my dad taught me to be self-sufficient. That's something I want to teach my kids. Now it's my turn to watch Jason and Ashley make their own mistakes.

"What will make me the happiest isn't that my kids become lawyers or doctors. I want them to learn to *think* for themselves. I want to know that they can exist without me. I want to give them courage to stand up for the things they believe in. The absolute last thing I want them to do when they grow up, is to lie down."

When there is pain
a child brings love.

When there is despair
a child brings hope.

When there is darkness
a child brings laughter.

When there is worry
a child brings peace.

And when there is uncertainty
a child brings purpose.

Chapter Four

LIVING WITH UNCERTAINTY

Lisa Jean Gonsalves never dated much in college. Actually, Lisa Jean never dated much—period. It was not that she wasn't good-looking. On the contrary, Lisa Jean was very good-looking, and she was equally intelligent. She just never believed in sex before marriage and, in the seventies, premarital sex was a popular option. However, it was never an option for Lisa Jean, and she was never high on the popularity polls of young men as a result.

In 1976, on the eve of her twenty-first birthday, Lisa Jean decided to do something different to celebrate. She went out for a drink with a good friend. One reason she chose to go out, however, was that her date was a policeman. She felt safe going out with a cop. Her parents didn't worry much, either. Richard wasn't just *any* motorcycle cop. Richard was an old friend of the family.

Lisa Jean's mother would often bring Richard hot coffee and crumb cake while he was on duty at their street corner. It was commonly known as a "duck pond stop" to other officers, and a "speed trap" to drivers. Although she lived in a rough neighborhood, Lisa Jean was totally at ease while being out late at night with a cop like Richard. Of course, the other reason to go out with Richard was that he was an absolute knockout. Lisa Jean had a mad crush on him ever since she could remember.

It was on that evening back '76 that Richard introduced Lisa Jean to her one and only true love. As it turned out, Richard was *also* as intelligent as he was good-looking. He had set up the meeting way in advance between Lisa Jean and his friend, Jimmy. Thankfully, Lisa Jean had no idea she was being set up.

The day after Lisa Jean's twenty-first birthday, Richard asked her if it was okay if he gave Jimmy her phone number. When she arrived home from work, her phone was ringing. Jimmy and Lisa Jean went out on their first date the evening after they were introduced. Their traditional romance continued for four years. Lisa Jean remembers the details as if it were yesterday.

"On our first date, Jimmy was an hour late because of traffic. We drove across town to see a prison movie called *Short Eyes*. It was a cop movie, of course. Then we went to a local hangout for a drink. I became more and more captivated with Jimmy as the evening progressed. I also felt like I was doing all the talking. That night I told my parents that I probably wouldn't go out with him again because he surely thought I talked too much.

"Two whole weeks passed before I heard from Jimmy again. Richard had already leaked it to me that Jimmy was going to ask me out to a Christmas dinner dance. I felt like I was back in high school waiting for the phone to ring. Sure enough, Jimmy called and asked me out again. I spent hours getting ready and, again, he was late. After an hour and a half of waiting, I figured I must have had the date wrong and went back upstairs and got undressed. As soon as I did, Jimmy was at my door.

"Two days before Christmas, Jimmy came over and gave me a small wrapped gift. I shouldn't have opened it until Christmas, but the minute he left, I unwrapped it and then wrapped it back up again. It was a necklace with a watch on it. I was caught totally off guard. In my book, giving jewelry is a serious statement. I went right out and got him an engraved St. Christopher's medal.

"Jimmy came over during his dinner break from work on Christmas Eve and I gave him my gift. I'll never forget him sitting at the supper table. He was wearing his shiny new St. Christopher's medal around his neck, and all my relatives kept staring at him while he tried to eat. I thought I'd never see him again."

But much to Lisa Jean's surprise, Jimmy called her at midnight on New Year's Eve. He had just dropped off his date, and he said it was the last time he ever wanted to date anyone else. "A few months later, I met his family. One of his brothers was a cop and the other two were federal prison guards. Other than that, they were just like every other close-knit family. His mom was especially kind and soft-spoken. I could tell that her sons had the deepest respect and admiration for her. I sensed that they'd do anything for her and had never, ever disappointed her. Though they didn't show it outwardly, you could just tell how deeply they all loved her and cared about each other. I was impressed.

"Jimmy and I dated for four years before we were married at a local church. We had the wedding I'd dreamed of all my life … a total of twenty bridesmaids and ushers, 550 guests, a ballroom reception, and a Caribbean cruise honeymoon."

Everything about Jimmy and Lisa Jean's romance was so traditional, it was almost like they were living a fairy tale. She had even saved her virginity for this man, her only love. By 1985, they were blessed with two children. Life could not get any better than that. Or so it seemed.

What was not traditional about this love affair was that Lisa Jean married a *cop*. They have remained happily married since their wedding day in 1982. That is something, unfortunately, not traditional in the life of a cop. There hasn't been one day without an extraordinary amount of stress in their life, and stress is all too traditional when you're married to a cop.

"Jimmy would leave for work on Sunday afternoon and we wouldn't see him again until 2:30 Thursday morning. I worked Monday, Tuesday, and Thursday while the kids stayed at my parents. Wednesday, I did 'wife and mother' things like grocery shopping and laundry. Friday was for Jimmy and me and Saturday was for the family. It was a good system, but I was always worried for his safety. He'd been in wrecks and was shot at several times.

"Some days I wished I'd married a plumber and that I worked in a flower shop doing crafts. We had so little time together and, even back then, I always wondered if he was okay. There were times I wanted out of the marriage. I wasn't used to that much stress in my life."

And as if this stress wasn't enough, after twenty years of patrol duty, Jimmy decided to accept a special five-year assignment doing undercover work for a drug task force. Lisa Jean had no idea of the definition of stress until the day Jimmy decided to go undercover.

"He called me from a phone booth and said that he had ten minutes to decide whether to take the assignment, but I could already tell that he had told them 'yes.'

"Jimmy's supervisors said his new job would be ten to six, Monday through Friday. What a crock! It's sixteen-hour days with little thanks, and we *never* see him Monday through Friday. Half the time he's not even in the state. He gets beeped at all hours, off days, vacation days, holidays—you name it. We can never plan any trips together. The kids have to attend a school far outside our county. We can't even go to a local movie or the malls together. Everything we do as a family has to be done far away where Jimmy is less apt to be recognized or seen with me and the kids. We don't even go to church together. At times it just seems unbearable."

More than four years have passed since Jimmy became an undercover narcotics agent. Today, an older and wiser Lisa Jean says, "I used to fight it, but now I've learned that it's all part of the job. Jimmy's a dedicated cop. It doesn't matter if he's on or off duty. If someone needs help, he responds. That's just the kind of person he is. And he truly believes he's making a difference in stopping the flow of illegal drugs into this country. If Jimmy says he is, then I'm behind him every step of the way.

"I consider myself a single mom Monday through Friday. Through all of this, I've learned to become a good listener and to have patience. Some days it's not so easy, but I'm a stronger person because of it. And we've both learned not to take each other for granted.

"Jimmy's safety is still foremost in the back of my mind. You never get used to that. I carry a beeper and he calls whenever he can to let me know he's okay. When the beeper goes off I shudder at first, because I'm never sure if it's Jimmy or his brother saying that I need to meet him at a hospital. Every time Jimmy calls, I remember to tell him that I love him. And when he finally comes home from work and I hear our garage door open, I always remember to say, 'Thank you, God.'"

Lisa Jean says that Jimmy's changed, too. "Having kids of our own has made his heart a little kinder. Sometimes he'll come home from work and tell me about a raid he did that day and that there were children in the house. When they had to break down the door, he'd see the kids in a corner, crying and scared half to death. It would be Jimmy, time after time, who'd make sure that the kids were taken care of. He'd comfort them like they were his own and feel terrible for the mess of a life they were in.

"Jimmy was rarely affectionate to kids before he had his own. The day after our daughter was born, he came home from work and went straight over to her cradle. He picked her up slowly and kissed her all over her little face and mouth. As I watched him, the tears streamed down my face. He had always been the strong one, the calm one, while I was the affectionate and outspoken one.

"Jimmy's different now, especially around kids—anyone's kids. There's something that happens when you become a parent. You feel a certain degree of empathy for *all* families and a responsibility to *all* children. That's the way Jimmy is now, and I think that's why he puts his life on the line every day in the war against drugs. I'll say to him, 'Jimmy, is it so important that you risk getting killed? Whether you live or die, you're not going to change the world.' He'll stare back at me and say, 'I know more than what you read in the newspapers. I *am* making a difference. We all are.'

"I'm proud of what Jimmy does, even though it's rough on our family. It's especially hard not having him home on holidays, like on Christmas when I'll have a house full of people. His brothers come over with a truckload of toys for the kids. We all eat early, and then Jimmy will have to run off in a hurry to work. But just before he leaves, he'll pull me off to the side. We'll sneak into a room and say our goodbyes. Then the tears start rolling down my face. Those are the times I especially hate.

"It's not easy on Jimmy, either. He lost his mom last year from ALS [Amyotrophic Lateral Sclerosis, commonly known as Lou Gehrig's Disease], and then right after that, an officer he'd been best friends with for the last sixteen years was shot and killed. That was almost harder on him than losing his mom. Totally out of character, he broke down and cried. I've never seen him do that before. For the first time ever, I held onto Jimmy and became the strong one.

"I think he realized then that he's *not* invincible, and it could have been him. He's fallen from a rooftop, been shot and beaten up, has had guns put to his head, he's crashed his car more than once, on and on … but until his best friend died on the job, Jimmy hadn't *really* thought much about death. I reminded him then and I remind him now, that his guardian angel is always on duty and is always looking out for him. I also tell him that I've put in a good word.

"A lot of people ask me how I do it. I don't know myself, but what I *do* know is that we have two wonderful kids to raise and that's what matters most of all. As we've grown a little older, we've learned to appreciate each other and our kids more and more every day. I think that's true with most families, not just ours. Families of police officers will always be different, though. We're dependent on each other for emotional support. I know other families, but it's never the same as ours.

"More than fifty percent of all police families I know are divorced, but I refuse to become part of that statistic. Even in the worst of times, I'm always thankful to hear our garage door open at 2:30 in the morning and my husband's footsteps coming through the door. Those are sounds that will always bring me peace."

Life is what happens to us while making other plans.

—Bev Wanlin

Chapter Five

CREDIBILITY AND CONVICTION

It's a safe bet that Margaret Virginia Traughber was a "strong willed" child. At age 78, she's probably the strongest willed LPN working today. If you're ever in need of health care, you'd want your nurse to be Margaret. Why? Because she'll be there for you. Never mind that it's snowing and only 15 degrees outside. Never mind that she's already put in a ten-hour work day. She'll be there. You have her word.

"I just do what needs to be done. The good Lord takes care of the rest."

When Margaret entered nursing school, she was 68 years old. "A lot of people said that I was too old and they would never take me. But I studied hard and I received a high enough score on the aptitude test that they couldn't turn me down."

In 1985, and fifty years older than her youngest classmate, Margaret graduated from the program and passed the State Board Exam as a Licensed Practical Nurse. What do people say now?

"I guess they know me by now, and they're not surprised. When all you hear are discouraging words, after a period of time you begin to believe them, and it can easily depress you. I never listened too long to that kind of talk. Instead, I believed in the excitement of possibilities. I chose to learn, and I worked hard at it. The key to success is found in education. Even when I was caring for my six younger brothers, I always made time for my studies."

As a child, Margaret probably colored outside the lines. She's more than spunky—she breaks the rules. When she was twenty-six, she took a job with Domestic Egg Products, Inc. as a Manager and Buyer, "when most women were rarely asked to think." After six months on the job, she had spent a million dollars, moved 118,935 cases of eggs, and supervised more than 200 employees. But after the end of World War II, the male employees returned home and Margaret was asked to take on different work "more in line with what women were doing in those days."

"The men who were working with me and under me resented my authority, and especially having to go through me for any money." Although by then she had seven years invested with the company, Margaret resigned in pursuit of another career. "Back in those days, women rarely had careers, let alone more than one. I guess you could say that I've never lived by the book, but you just can't stand there and let people run all over you."

Margaret returned to school and became a successful life insurance agent, only to realize that she was happiest when she cared for others. "It just seemed natural for me to care for children after all those years of caring for my siblings."

She changed gears and became a live-in nanny, caring for a four-month-old boy. One afternoon, Margaret and the boy's mother were sipping tea on the front porch while he was asleep in his buggy, enjoying the light summer breeze. His mother had just checked on him and gone into the house while Margaret prepared his noon feeding. Suddenly, Margaret felt something was wrong, and she decided to check on him herself. She found him lifeless, suffocating in his sheet and turning blue. Margaret immediately began using mouth-to-mouth resuscitation, and she and his mother rushed him to the doctor.

Margaret saved a life that afternoon and she decided that there was nothing more important than the well-being and care of another person. For the next ten days, the infant slept on her shoulder rather than in his crib until Margaret felt comfortable leaving him alone again. "Looking back, I realize that God had a plan for me that afternoon that I knew nothing about."

In 1979, Margaret became "House Mother" for Vanderbilt University's Kappa Alpha Theta Sorority House, a job she enjoyed until she made a "fatal" decision that got her fired. Margaret broke the rules once again. She hired a black man as a cook for the young sorority women.

"What if he sees the girls in improper attire?" her superior argued.

"They won't be improperly attired on that floor as long as I'm in charge."

"But it's against the rules, Margaret."

"I can't be bothered with rules when they serve no purpose," said Margaret.

"Well, they showed me the door, but I'm still proud of the choice I made. They did keep him on, mind you, and he's still cooking their meals today. The girls all love that man, too. He's become a father to them. They come back year after year to show him their babies."

While most people in their sixties are thinking about retiring, Margaret wanted a license to practice nursing. She went back to school and earned her nursing degree and license to care for others. She's been a working LPN for the last ten years, taking care of men and women—mostly her age—in nursing home facilities with over forty beds.

"I like caring for others. It's not about slinging pills. It's about looking into someone's eyes and telling them not to worry because I'll be there to take care of them. If I got sick, I'd want to know that I had someone who cared to take care of me. That alone brings about peace and faster recovery. The first thing I do is give them my word." And Margaret's reassuring word is what most anyone needs.

"I was brought up with values of kindness, truth, and honesty. I find people are still like that. Especially when I go back home to Bedford County, Tennessee. I may not have a lot of riches, but I have lots of family and friends … and my education. These are the things that really matter."

Against the advice of her family members and friends, Margaret still drives the annual 1,500-mile journey home from southern Kansas. She makes the trip with only her two cats to keep her company, and in a car which has well over 100,000 miles on it. Once again, Margaret breaks the rules and, again, she could never be stopped. Amused that anyone should worry, she smiles quickly and adds, "It's a Buick."

That's the way her life has been. Whenever Margaret heard the word "stop," she would "go" even faster. Back at the ripe young age of 57, Margaret not only married, she married a man sixteen years younger than herself. "In the forties, all the men were gone to war, and the ones left, I didn't want. So I remained single until I was 57. I am not sure Jim was thinking of marriage when he asked a friend for my phone number, but eighteen months later, we married. It may have taken awhile, but he really did convince me that age didn't matter.

"Age is only a reflection in the mirror. I'm just about eighty years old now. I have one daughter, three step-children, three foster children, plenty of grandchildren, and even a great granddaughter. The Lord provides me with my daily bread, and then some. I have a good place to live and work and I have lots of friends, some I've just met, and some I've known for thirty, forty, fifty, and sixty years. That ain't so bad."

Look into life's mirror
and learn from what you see.

Chapter Six

LEARN FROM ONE ANOTHER

Will's story is not a very happy one. Some view his life as tragic, while others— including Will—do not. Will has shared his story so that people may learn something from his life. He wants his life to continue to serve some purpose.

Will R. Field has never been an average Joe, and he's the first to admit it. He is also the first to admit that the clock is ticking and, until recently, he has not used his time wisely. Although his remaining time may be little, his goals have grown big.

Will attends college full time because he needs more than just a BS degree in Elementary Education. He wants to become a substance abuse counselor specializing in the HIV virus and AIDS. As a counselor, Will hopes to help others cope with and accept their mistakes, or perhaps prevent someone from making the same wrong turns that he has made.

Will is paying for his bad choices in life with his health. He suffers from chronic fatigue and migraines, but he said that he is "getting along." In 1985, Will was diagnosed HIV positive and he was given approximately five years to live. Considering his lifestyle and history of drug addiction, the news came as no surprise to Will. He has accepted his ill fate, although he never has accepted the "five-year plan." Besides his career goals, Will has discovered his own purpose in life. His biggest regret is that it's taken him forty years to realize it.

Will was raised in a seemingly "normal," upper-class, two-parent family with five children. His father was a teacher and college chancellor. His mother was a homemaker and nurse. He grew up in Minnesota like hundreds of other kids, playing softball in neighborhood parks and going to birthday parties with lots of balloons and funny hats.

"Good parenting skills were practiced during my childhood," said Will. "I don't blame my circumstances on my parents. In fact, I'm grateful to them for my upbringing and education." Will loves his parents, and he often tells them so. He believes that his parents "were pretty good after all," and that the big mistakes he made during his teenage years and later on were his own responsibility.

Although Will was a "loner" as an adolescent, he was a "fairly typical" teen. "I wanted to learn, but I also wanted instant gratification. I constantly struggled with the questions of 'who I am' and 'where I belonged' before considering where I was headed. I took life for granted and thought I was invincible most of the time." That sounds like a lot of young people. The difference, however, was that Will began using drugs at age fourteen.

Will served in the Air Force during the Vietnam era. He was twenty-one when he enlisted. Now, he's a Disabled Vet. He was first married and divorced during the seventies, and his only child from that marriage died when he was only two years old. Will frequently used drugs to escape his problems and he eventually sought out treatment.

After he completed his drug treatment program for a second time, Will remarried in 1985. His new wife was from a wealthy, upper-class family, and she had two daughters from a previous marriage. "Our marriage was like a roller coaster ride," said Will, "and not unlike my life." For two years of their eight-year marriage, he and his wife were separated. Today, they are back together. "She's still there when I'm having a tough time. She's my best friend, but we also need our 'Time-Outs' from each other."

Starting in 1991, Mr. and Mrs. Will R. Field were homeless for eighteen months. They had little money, no jobs, and were in poor health. "Being homeless was difficult, but it was not my biggest or sole challenge in life." Will also struggled with his hot temper and violent tendencies. He sometimes physically abused his wife. His stepchildren entered a foster home where they remain today. They maintain a fragile and strained relationship with Will and their mother.

Acknowledging his problems, Will sought treatment through a men's domestic abuse program. Now, three years later, Will's emotional life is more balanced. His visits with his stepdaughters are still infrequent, but their relationship is improving. "We've all grown and changed over the years. The girls are thirteen and sixteen years old now. Today I get along with them better than their mother does. I miss them and care for them deeply. Even though they are in foster care, the girls are stable now and that's what matters."

In 1993, Will's wife and "best friend" was diagnosed with Multiple Personality Disorder. In addition, she and Will remain unsure whether or not she has contracted the HIV virus because of fluctuating test results, a situation his wife said is not unheard of among women. To make matters worse, two of her brothers were diagnosed with AIDS—one has died already and the other is in the process of dying. Although Will and his wife came from "fairly well-off" families, Will knows that, "there are no free rides or guarantees in life—everything comes with a price."

Will's mistakes and subsequent problems seem never-ending. He admits that "mirrors aren't real friendly," and that it's taken him most of his life to examine his behavior and confront reality. Will has been "clean" for almost ten years, and now he faces his daily challenges head-on. "My wife is the sparkle in my life. I couldn't live without her. I'm also very concerned for her. She's been there for me during the difficult, abusive times. I worry about not being there for her, too." Living with HIV, Will knows that in time, his wife may have to live without him.

"But my life finally has a purpose. I want to help others, like myself, who have made bad choices in life." After all is said and done, Will Field is more concerned about others than he is about himself and his being HIV positive. "There are others trying to cope with things more terrible than this."

As a counselor, Will hopes to "speak from experience and remind others to use each day wisely." His counseling agenda for future clients will focus on living, not dying, while learning to cope with the consequences of personal actions. From this platform, he wants to speak to those who have also made some big mistakes in life and to others who just want to listen. "The world needs more listeners and more *caring*," he said.

"It's easy not to care or not to love. And it's very easy to give up. *Anyone* can give up. It's a hard struggle, but once you're clean, you can have an open mind. Life is exciting when you're clean and it can get even better. Everyone makes their own mistakes. The key is to learn from them so you don't make the same mistakes twice. Sometimes you don't get a second chance." This is the advice from a man who has run out of second chances.

Will's father, like other fathers, always wanted his children to become successful in life. His son chose a different road, but like his father, Will has also become a teacher and someone to learn from. With every new day that he is blessed, Will Field looks forward to helping someone else. He will give back the blessing of life by giving hope to the hopeless, and "by making a difference in the life of someone who's less fortunate than myself."

With the goal of counseling others, Will has found that his life has purpose after all. "Eventually we all find a purpose as to why we are here. For some like myself, it takes a little longer than for others."

I've come to think of the world
as a big pot of soup.
If all you have is the stock,
it's a very bland pot of soup.

Once the vegetables are added,
the soup takes on some
flavor and character.

But it's not until you add the salt,
pepper, garlic, bay leaves, oregano, and basil
that the soup comes alive.

—Nancy Libby

Chapter Seven

LEAVING THE PREJUDICE BEHIND

For fifteen years, Spud, as he was fondly called, was not only a surrogate child, he was the only child of Nancy and Bart Libby. He was different from the neighbors' children because Spud was "biracial." Often he endured names such as "half-breed" and "mutt." At times the name-calling hurt his pride, but Spud's parents were proud of his mixed background.

Nancy was a hairstylist by trade. Although Spud was a male, she routinely spent hours washing, cutting, and styling her son's curly, kinky locks until he pranced around the kitchen with joy. Like most boys his age, Spud despised taking baths, but he loved to have his mother dote on him, and he looked forward to the attention he received from her. When she was done, he'd fall asleep in front of the fireplace until his little body was toasty warm, almost too warm to touch. Spud led the kind of life that some people only dream about.

Nancy never could understand why some of her closest friends didn't love Spud the way she did. In spite of how deeply affectionate he was, and no matter how cute or well-behaved Spud acted, some of her family and friends just didn't like Spud very much. Maybe he was a little strange to them because he was different in some ways. Of course, one can't expect other people to love a child the way his mother does, no matter what. Then again, some people just don't like dogs. Nevertheless, Spud was one lucky dog.

In January 1990, shortly after his fifteenth birthday, Spud suddenly became seriously ill and he died in his sleep. The ground was too frozen and snowcovered for his father to bury him in the back yard. Bart and Nancy said their last goodbyes, and the local vet took care of his remains. When the ground thawed in spring, they buried Spud's collar, tags, and favorite toys. It was a long winter in 1990 and a very dark time for the Libbys.

People can grow just as attached to animals as parents are to their children. Raising a pet from birth through adulthood and beyond is like living a condensed version of parenthood. Spud was alive for fifteen of Bart and Nancy's twenty years of marriage, and memories of Spud will remain with them forever. He received a stable upbringing in a functional two-parent family. Until the winter Spud passed away, he lived his entire life in the same neighborhood, chasing the same cats.

Spud heard his parents love, laugh, and cry together. He watched them save their money for years to pay for their dream house. He saw them toil over cutting the ceramic tiles for the entry way and argue over selecting the granite for their handmade woodstove hearth. Spud watched as they moved into a custom home that Bart and Nancy designed and practically built themselves on several acres of land in California's Sierra Nevada Mountains. It was only three weeks after their move when Spud died.

The Libbys seemed to have everything, so why were they so sad about their pet? A parent knows exactly why. They had lost their "only child." And throughout their marriage, Nancy and Bart did everything possible, but they still could not conceive a child.

"We spent many, many years taking infertility tests, being inseminated, taking my temperature, and taking drugs to treat whatever it was that may have needed treating. Yet we still suffered the disappointment of failure month after month, year after year. Then we realized that this baby business was simply out of our hands. Obviously the timing was not up to us," said Nancy.

"It got to a point where we simply decided to trust God for what was best for our lives," added Bart.

As much as she tried to put the issue to rest however, Nancy felt depressed. Still devastated by the loss of their dog, she was lonely and confused.

"I felt that my life had lost purpose. Although my faith in God was strong, I was stuck in a season of despair. I knew I had so much to give, but I didn't know *how* to give or where. I kept asking God how I could be useful and I tried my best to remain patient.

"That winter was an especially rough time for us. We cried buckets and confided in one another that we just could not go on living in anticipation of every month for what remained of our childbearing years. I guess we reluctantly gave up the idea of having a child of our own. We had toyed with the idea of adoption, but we could never agree on when to begin the paperwork or even where to go to do it. Adoption seemed like such a maze of confusion to us. We decided to put the whole issue of having a child on the back burner and simply live our lives for a while."

Bart was traveling in Florida with a Christian music ministry when he called home one day. Nancy asked him a question that drew a surprising response. "I asked Bart if he felt he was in God's perfect will working as a musician in this ministry. Something inside me said that he should be home. Bart thought about it, and then he answered, 'Not God's *perfect* will, but His permissive will.' " Having said that, Bart agreed to quit his traveling. And that's when it happened—within two weeks of Bart's return home, and just two months after Spud had died, Nancy became pregnant for the first time. She was thirty-nine years old.

"After what seemed like an eternity of depression, we became absolutely jubilant!" Nancy was actually a little *sick* and jubilant.

"Of course, at my age, the doctor wanted to do an amniocentesis. I clearly told him that I had waited too long for this child, and that I would accept whatever package God chose to send me." In January 1991, Bart and Nancy's long-awaited "package" finally arrived. Nancy gave birth to a beautiful boy they named Evan, meaning "God's gracious gift."

At first, parenthood was "overwhelming" for Bart and Nancy, like it is for most new parents, no matter what their age. "It was such an unfamiliar position to be in! Suddenly, I found that I had not one minute for myself, let alone for Bart and me together. I was routinely having to get up from my desperately-needed sleep to feed this little person whom I didn't even know! I couldn't believe Evan needed so much care from his exhausted mother."

While Evan's parents were stressed and in need of sleep, their newborn son was doing just great. Well-wishers dropped in at all hours of the day and night to take a "peek" and give their hearty congratulations. All seemed "normal" in the new Libby household.

Evan was an unusually passive and quiet baby. In fact, other mothers were a little envious of how undemanding he was compared to their own newborns. As the months passed and Evan grew older, Nancy began to make comparisons, as many mothers do. That is when she began to notice differences in Evan's abilities that became causes for concern.

"At six months of age, Evan was still unable to hold his head up strong, like other kids. He did not roll over on the same schedule as other kids, either. And he was not sitting up at all. We began to worry and consulted our local pediatrician, only to be told that all was fine. Unsatisfied, I went to the local Health Department, and a very knowledgeable nurse practitioner spotted something peculiar in Evan. Not only did Evan's muscle tone appear weak, she confirmed our suspicions that Evan was lagging far behind in the normal development of a toddler. She suggested further testing for a specific diagnosis.

"In the year that followed, we saw hearing specialists, ophthalmologists, geneticists, neurologists, orthopedic specialists, and a wide range of related professionals in between. Finally, after having an MRI performed when Evan was eighteen months old, the doctors discovered that our son had a very rare disorder known in the medical field as 'Dandy/Walker Syndrome.'

"For a good while, Bart and I were completely devastated. Never in our lives did we have to deal with information like this. You always think of these things happening to other people. Our minds raced, wondering what life would be like and how we would cope further down the road. Would our son ever be like other children? More importantly, would he be *liked* by other children? Would he play ball or learn to ski? Would he ever learn to read? Would he even be able to speak or perform simple tasks like feed himself? And if not, what *was* his real potential?" Nancy and Bart's questions and concerns were endless.

"We had absolutely no idea what life had in store for us. The world was spinning out of control. And where was God? How could He do this to us, I thought, after we waited so long for our child?"

Nancy tried to accept their son's diagnosis, but not much made sense to her. "First, I had to face my previous prejudices toward disabled people of all kinds. After gallons of tears and many late night talks with Bart, I began the process all parents go through to accept a birth defect. You grieve the loss of the person you thought your child might be, and then you begin to accept who they really are. It isn't easy, but it *must* happen if you are to have a rich life with your child.

"But as time passed, Bart and I began to see what a blessing our son is, as are all children. Special needs children, in particular, are truly gifts to us all. I've come to think of the world as a big pot of soup. If all you have is the stock, it's a very bland pot of soup. Once the vegetables are added, the soup takes on some flavor and character. But it's not until you add the salt, pepper, garlic, bay leaves, oregano, and basil that the soup comes *alive*. Special needs kids are the spice of life. Similarly, adults with disabilities contribute to society in more ways than they ever realize."

That's not to say that raising a special needs child is an easy task. The demands on any parent are great, but Nancy discovered challenges far beyond what she ever imagined or thought possible of her.

"The parents of special needs children are special people themselves. Take the time to get to know them and their children and you'll find yourself blessed, enlightened, and changed forever. I believe God uses special people as our teachers to improve upon our character and keep us focused on the important things in life. Bart and I have learned to appreciate things that we once took for granted, simple things that we were too busy to see before. Evan has also made me a stronger person. Now I have a sense of direction and purpose in my everyday life.

"I've learned that the need to be assertive and organized is imperative to the well-being of our son. I am not only his mother, I am his *voice*. I know when he's uncomfortable, even though he will never complain. After Evan recently had surgery, for example, I insisted that he be given pain medication although the nurse thought otherwise because Evan doesn't verbalize like other toddlers. The medication enabled him to get the rest he desperately needed. Parents need to speak up for their children to insure that they have the best care and education possible.

"My other big challenge lies in the fact that our nearest major medical center is one hundred miles from our home. This means that Evan's appointments must be carefully scheduled, checked and rechecked and, whether there is a blizzard or not, my promptness is paramount. I thank my parents for raising me to be a responsible person because without that quality, our son would suffer. It's been a huge challenge to be the mother of a child with multiple disabilities, but it's also an honor that is humbling to accept.

"Life is never what you think it might be, and the uncertainty can be somewhat scary. There was a time not too long ago when I thought I could continue my career *and* give our son all the nurturing and special care he deserves. By the time Evan turned two years old, however, Bart and I discovered we were running ourselves ragged juggling two work schedules around our domestic life. We mutually decided it was time for me to stop working outside the home. Evan needed more time and attention than what we were giving him, and *he* is our priority.

"I quit my job with no regrets, and soon after that, Evan and I went to spend some time at his grandparents. While sleeping in the same room with Ev, I noticed that he was having trouble breathing while he slept.

"He underwent yet another series of tests and was diagnosed with 'Obstructive Sleep Apnea,' a condition that causes the sleeper to stop breathing several times a night. Surgery corrected this condition, but if I hadn't spent several days with Evan at my parents' house, I would have missed the opportunity to detect Evan's problem. Unbeknownst to us, our son was in trouble, and we could very well have lost him."

Nancy has learned many lessons from her son. Evan has taught her to be strong, to have patience and compassion, to learn acceptance, and—Nancy's greatest lesson of all—to have a purpose in life.

"The uncertainty aspect of life is the hardest of all to accept. I've relied heavily on a saying I once heard: We do not know what the future holds, but we know who holds the future. Now I have a much greater dependence on God than ever before. I've found that for me, a life not lived for oneself is a life much more fulfilling. If I had wanted to change my character into a more compassionate and understanding person, one that was not repelled by disabled people, I could never have dreamed up a better method than being Evan's mother."

"Through all of our ups and downs together over the last twenty-five years," said Bart, "it's been reassuring and comforting to remember that Evan's life is not an accident. He is a gift to us from God, and he has enriched our lives beyond measure."

It used to be that Spud was the lucky one to have parents like Bart and Nancy Libby. The world has become richer since the long, difficult winter of 1990. The tables have turned with the seasons. "We're the lucky ones now," said Nancy, "to have been blessed with such a special son like Evan.

"Evan is here for a purpose, as is every life conceived. I speak from experience when I say that these are precious lives that need to come into the world to bless and flavor it. Never could I have had a greater teacher in life than our son. I have truly never known a person with such a sweet and gentle spirit. I would feel cheated had I never known Evan."

The stone that holds up the sky
can be the same stone
that blocks the road.

Become a foundation of support
rather than a wall
that divides.

Chapter Eight

BECOME YOUR CHILD'S BEST ADVOCATE

Nancy Crump Ford is a teacher, wife, and the mother of two daughters. Every day in the classroom, she saw students who hated school. Having her own children grow up hating school was her biggest fear as a parent. It's also what motivated her to teach her children at home.

"Kids should love learning as an ongoing aspect of life, not just during certain hours. I saw kids being influenced in good and bad ways early in their lives and I thought, Why not be actively involved in Sara and Megan's development? It's not only my right as their mother, it's my job as their parent."

This is the philosophy which motivated Nancy to accept the responsibility of educating her two daughters at home. She home-schooled them for five of their early learning and formative years. Home teaching is an alternate method of education that does not require a teaching degree or professional background in education. Nancy was a licensed teacher when she began home teaching. She said, however, that "the heart of a teacher and the unconditional love of a parent is what's needed to home teach—not an academic degree.

"My husband and I both wanted our girls to have the best opportunity for building as solid a foundation as possible. Our biggest fear was that they would lose their love of learning and ultimately get lost in the public school system. There are far too many illiterate kids graduating from high school. As parents, we felt accountable for our children's educational well-being and character development."

For the next five years, Nancy "laid down her life" to educate her children. "It was a labor of love, but I can honestly say that those were the happiest years of my life."

Megan and Sara started their home schooling in kindergarten and ended after completing their second and fourth grades, respectively. After that, they were mainstreamed into a small private school for two years and then into the Virginia public school system. The girls are teenagers now, and they have tested above normal academically for their grade levels.

Nancy customized her daughters' curriculum, and she admits that it took a certain degree of experimentation to discover the right ingredients.

"I did a lot of research and tried three phonics programs before finding one that worked for us. First, I concentrated on the language arts—phonics, spelling, and vocabulary. Once our girls learned to read, I added math, English, science, and history."

Entertainment was not a part of Nancy's curriculum. "I literally removed our television from the house for all five years. We had a strict schedule of lessons for three to four hours every morning that included one nap or rest period. In reality, only four hours a day is spent learning in formal classroom settings. One of the great things about home schooling is that you can be flexible which, after all, makes for a well-balanced life. Of course, working one-on-one with my children also provided them the opportunity to finish school by noon, which *they* enjoyed."

Nancy encouraged a "hands-on" method of learning. "To make learning a memorable and real-life experience, we went on field trips with a half dozen other home schooling families two or three times each month. It's very important to network with other families in your area. It allows you to pool your resources and provide a well-rounded learning environment. In a group, we would visit hospitals, historical sites, museums, the symphony, and various artists. Every trip was related to the units we were currently studying. Once, we even dissected a fetal pig on my kitchen table!

"These outings also provide your children with the opportunity to develop social skills in small group settings that carry over into later years. It's a wonderfully enriched curriculum without limits. You can be as creative as you want to be."

Nancy's field trips also included retirement homes where her children could learn firsthand from the residents. "Our youngest daughter, Megan, still visits a nursing home on her own initiative. She views some of the elderly residents as her dearest of friends. One of the lessons she has learned through their special friendship is that the greatest gift to give someone is unconditional love."

Nancy also recommends becoming a host family to foreign exchange students. "By hosting foreign students, your family can learn directly about different languages and customs from a variety of other cultures."

For Nancy, there were many other obvious advantages of home schooling.

Nancy took comfort in knowing that she wasn't completely alone as a teacher to her children. She developed her curriculum from a shared base of knowledge and resources among networks of professional people and other home schooling families.

"It's really a help to know you are not alone. We all gave each other a strong degree of support. The other perk, of course, was that we could plan our vacations during the off-season and get good rates while avoiding the crowds!"

This is not to say that home teaching isn't without its own set of unique challenges to conquer. "It's imperative that you stick to a routine and a specific schedule, and that lessons are planned and adhered to. There's an old saying, 'If you fail to plan, you plan to fail.' That couldn't be more true with home schooling. You definitely need all your ducks in a row and then stick to your daily lesson plans, with no wasted time in between."

Nancy had an additional challenge with teaching her children. One daughter was diagnosed with Attention Deficit Disorder, commonly called "ADD."

"Our youngest daughter had problems processing information. She was developing a low self-esteem when we detected her learning disability. I think she definitely would have been lost in the system or simply termed 'strong-willed' or 'rebellious' had I not been there to catch it early. It's so critical that you catch a student's mistakes or more serious learning disorders early. Having a one-on-one teaching relationship with my daughter allowed me to work patiently with her. We worked in five-minute intervals, and I kept her off the widely-used medications. I compensated for her deficiency and used other ways for her to learn the material. By age eight, she was reading very well on her own. Most teaching provides a slow result, but I got an immediate positive response from our daughter. She's her own person and she is doing absolutely great in school now. I feel so fortunate to live in a country where we have a choice in the education of our children."

Fortunately for Nancy's children, and especially her youngest child, she chose to "be there" for them. Home teaching isn't an easy task. Nancy admits that there were times when they all ended up in tears. You have to be loving, dedicated and, most of all, able to keep things in perspective.

"I had to keep reminding myself that my kids should enjoy the learning process, enjoy the ride. There were no grades given, and I never criticized their mistakes. We're all students in life. I used a motto that mistakes are our friends and they are vehicles for learning."

Nancy's incentives were simple, like walks in the park, trips to the library, and free time. "We also read a lot. Sara and Megan would select a book and we'd read a chapter each night together. We shared simple family fun, like playing board games and activities that we all enjoyed doing.

"Look back at our experience, I learned that you have to become your child's best advocate. It's your right and priviledge as a parent to ensure the best care possible for your children. If you don't, then who will? Who cares about your children more than you? Who knows better what is best for their well-being?

"Parents are as smart as many college graduates. If you'd like to explore home teaching, read up on educational methods and research. Contact your local school superintendent for your own state's home teaching requirements. Then, pool your resources and network with other families. Home teaching is a constant challenge, but your kids are worth the investment."

Every parent wants their child to be successful in life, but Nancy has a different perspective now that she has home-taught her daughters. "Success is not about getting straight A's in school. It's about one's character and learning attributes such as respect, self-esteem, honesty, and caring for others. I watched our girls develop integrity and characters unique to each of them, as well as a solid foundation of academics. Then, I sat back and watched them take off on their own and blossom. They are capable of doing absolutely anything. Their potentials are as unique and strong as their characters."

Nancy gave her children a most precious gift—herself. She encouraged her daughters to learn, and then she became a witness to their achievements. For parents, there is nothing better than watching their children grow up well. Nancy knows this from experience, but she also knows something her daughters *don't* know—Sara and Megan gave her the best years of her life.

Just the other day, I noticed Alex's head and eyes
peering over the breakfast bar in our kitchen.
It seems that just a few months ago,
barely the top of his head was visible.
Time passes and it never returns.
Sometimes when he's asleep,
I'll go sit next to him and just watch him.
He won't be the same tomorrow.
He's more than someone special. He's my son.

—Gary Leonard Chandler

Chapter Nine

PRIORITIES AND THE TIES THAT BIND

Fatherhood is alive and well in rural North Carolina. In a time when it seems as though every other parent is an only parent, it's reassuring to know that parents like Gary Leonard Chandler still exist. Gary isn't a single parent, but he is one of the many great examples of fatherhood today.

Gary and his wife, Linda, have been married since 1980. It was the second marriage for both, and perhaps that fact alone contributed more than others to their priorities for planning a family. Gary was introduced to the reality of single parenting during his adolescence. He was thirteen years old when the greatest influence in his life, his sister Josephine, was divorced at age twenty-five. Josephine raised her three young daughters alone, and she also earned a master's degree and a doctorate at the same time.

"Josephine has always been my biggest role model, but at age thirteen, I had no idea of the magnitude of her achievements, either as an academician or a parent. It takes time and mistakes to realize those accomplishments. Now that I am a parent and forty-five years old, I look back at how Josephine persevered and what she undertook as a single parent at twenty-five, and I have to ask myself, What drove her? What inspired her?"

Fortunately for Gary, he doesn't have to be a single parent like his sister. His wife, Linda, is at the center of their relationship. But the most fortunate of all is Gary and Linda's five-year-old son, Alex.

Eight years ago, Gary survived a heart attack and three years later, at age thirty-nine, he underwent successful bypass surgery. Linda was nearly nine months pregnant at the time of Gary's surgery. Some people say your life is changed forever if you survive a heart attack. For Gary, his life changed the most during the month following his surgery, when Alex Garison Chandler was born. It was a tough time for Gary, but he says it was harder on his wife. It was a time neither will forget—the best of times and the worst of times.

"I literally thought my life was at an end, but Linda figuratively and often literally carried me through it. Even today when I get mad at her, I remember February 7, 1988, and there she was … physically exhausted while caring for our newborn son, and also encouraging me to get up and going with my rehabilitation. For Linda, I guess it was a time of birth and rebirth, as if she'd had twins."

For Gary, it was a time when he learned the true meaning of love and commitment. And it was with this same dedication that he and Linda entered into their new role as parents.

"We had thought so much and waited so long to become parents. Neither of us was sure that we would be good parents, most of all me. We had delayed starting a family for eight years while Linda put me through doctoral studies. After my education was complete, we both found good jobs in a town in which we felt comfortable raising a family. Then it came down to the question, 'How do we ensure that we'll be good parents?' After all, there's no test, no license required, no rule book to follow, and no guarantees. We both felt that it was a sacred trust, and we placed our faith in God."

A matter of trust is not always such a simple thing, and no one knows this better than Gary. He has trust in God for giving him a wonderful and committed wife, a second chance in life, and now a wonderful son. He trusts his marriage and never takes it for granted. He trusts his knowledge and the opportunities it has provided him as a college professor of health and physical education. And he trusts his roots and feels secure in the upbringing he's had. Gary holds his childhood memories in such high regard, that he and Linda returned to North Carolina to bring up their son just three and a half hours from the towns were they were raised. Gary has happy memories of growing up near the Blue Ridge Mountains. Now he hopes that Alex will fondly remember his "good ol' days" living in the foothills of those same peaks.

"There's not a lot to do in our small town, but then again, you don't get shot at much, either. The Western region is a great place to live and, we think, to grow up. From the sand spur still lodged in the sole of my foot to the barbecue between my teeth, North Carolina is my home in every sense of the word.

"You really have to wonder about the daily environment you are providing as a parent. In our town, everyone is the same. No matter what color your skin or what you do for a living, you're still someone special living here. My mama raised me with a saying I'll always remember. She said, 'Everybody has a soul. Everybody is important in God's eyes.' That's pretty much the way it is here. Townspeople still care about each other. You see old tobacco barns, clapboard houses, sandy roads leading who-knows-where … lots of country places with their history deep in the sandy soil. Places like Barbecue Church and Cape Fear Church, places that have withstood the test of time. Rural America truly is a special place to raise your family.

"When I was young and sometimes bored, I thought I lived in a 'hick' town. Now I think it might be getting a bit crowded here sometimes. I think it's important to never forget 'from whence we came,' and I want to build on what my parents taught me and pass it on to Alex. All our learning and traditions begin in childhood. I've learned that the reality of childhood is what we *remember* of it. Unfortunately, this applies to good *and* bad memories. I guess maybe I'll know someday when I hold my grandchild in my lap. As corny as it may sound, that's how we make a difference, one day at a time, one act at a time. We can either make a change for the better or for the worse.

"My number one lesson for Alex to learn now is that he is a member of the Chandler family, and that stands for something. It means that he must begin to carry his own weight and be responsible for his actions. Someday, part of this responsibility will be in passing on what he has learned to someone else. He is only five years old, but he already knows better than to blame someone else for his own mistakes. And whether he knows it or not, he's already passing on our love and respect for others every day to his friends at kindergarten.

"I guess Linda and I thought about things like this even before we named our son. When we were considering what to call him, we had many thoughts and struggles over the name that would give our child the best start in life. We decided upon *Alex* because its Old English meaning is *helper of mankind*. Linda and I could think of no more beneficial challenge to give our son. We also hoped that this would provide many instances for encouraging him to behave in positive ways as he was developing as a person.

"Linda allowed me the privilege of giving him the middle name of *Garison*, a variation of *Gary's son*, and hopefully that will be a positive influence in his life. We decided this as we sat on my hospital recovery bed, not many days after my surgery. Sometimes I think my son's middle name is the most vain thing I have ever done in my life. But sometimes I think of it as the one act filled with the most responsibility I have ever taken upon myself. Nonetheless, I hope he is ultimately half as proud as I am of it."

Not long ago, Gary and Linda moved Alex from one day-care facility to another. They felt that the new facility was more representative of the real world. In the end, they felt it was a healthier environment in which Alex could develop.

"We made the change primarily because of better racial blending. During our frequent visits, we saw that our own positive perceptions of people were being reinforced there. Still, even at his young age, Alex had some strong ties to his old friends which made this move a more difficult change for him. At first he felt alone in his new classroom of strangers, and it was hard for him to make friends. He'd come home crying and we'd want to cry, too. Linda said that maybe we'd made a mistake in moving him, but I wanted him to feel and accept the challenge that was before him. So we challenged him. We continued to give him our encouragement and support, and then we watched him rise to the occasion. It wasn't an easy lesson for any of us, but now Alex knows how to make him a buddy.

"One day not long after he started his new day care, he and I were talking about some things he had been doing at school with his new friends. Since I had not gotten to the point where I could recognize his friends by name, much less sight, I asked Alex who his friend Jason was that he had been playing with and talking so joyfully about. He said, 'Oh, he's the boy with the brown skin and he's my friend.' It was worth a month's day-care tuition just to hear him respond that way in a world that is too often racially torn and sometimes violently divided. Perhaps we *had* made the right choice. My mom *was* right. Everyone *does* have a soul, and two little boys on a playground proved it once again."

Gary never had his son's sense of self-esteem as a child, but he is learning it as a parent. "Another thing I never expected as a parent was having a new sense of purpose in life. I've channeled all my energy and courage into becoming the best parent I can. It's true that Alex has changed our lives in many ways we never expected, but we've never, ever regretted it. He's made better people of both of us. I guess he's made us more responsible in the same ways that we want him to be more responsible. I love being a teacher, and I'm probably an over-achiever. But Alex has taught me that other things in life do exist. I used to be a workaholic. I still bust my buns when I'm at work, but when I shut my office door behind me, I *leave* it all behind. My time away from work belongs to my family. Life is too short.

"Just the other day, I noticed Alex's head and eyes peering over the breakfast bar in our kitchen. It seems that just a few months ago, barely the top of his head was visible. Sometimes at work I look up at Alex's pictures on my wall and I see how he has grown in these past few months. Next year he'll be in full-time school. It's times like these that I literally drop what I'm doing and go pick him up from day care just to be near him. Time passes and it never returns. Sometimes when he's asleep, I'll go sit next to him and just watch him. He won't be the same tomorrow. He's more than someone special. He's my son.

"This summer we went to about a dozen Atlanta Braves' games as a family. I didn't get to do things like that as a kid, and I certainly didn't have a say-so in the matter. Alex is a part of all our decisions. He gets a vote. He has a choice. He's an individual. He's a person. Any family outings we had in my youth were usually preceded by, 'Get in the car …,' and not, 'Where do you want to go?'

"We really didn't take family vacations when I was growing up, so I started two new Chandler family traditions with Alex. Just before each Christmas, Linda, Alex, and I rent a rustic, wood-heated cabin for a couple days near Roan Mountain. Just the three of us. Our first time there, when Alex was a baby, it was twelve degrees below zero. Somehow, we saw this as a challenge to forge the continuing tradition, and we've been back every year since that first trip."

The second tradition began when Gary was a college student. "Backpacking is one of the main ways I get away and stay in touch with who I am." Gary has been backpacking most of his life, introducing hundreds of junior high and now college students to the wonders of nature and self-challenge.

"I guess all this was in preparation for the same type of opportunities with Alex, because he and another friend of mine recently went on a backpacking and camping trip, Alex's first. It started with Alex, at the age of two, hiking to the top of Table Rock, overlooking the Linville Gorge Wilderness Area. I was amazed, and I saw that even then, Alex was probably going to share my love for hiking and backpacking.

"I've been on the trails for nearly twenty-five years, but I don't think it ever has been more gratifying than now when Alex accompanies me. I love seeing his interest grow while knowing that I can share what I've learned with him. Everyone should be able to share these sorts of experiences."

And likewise, everybody should come to know the love between a father and his son. Alex is five years old, and he is already beginning to shoulder his own load. He seems never to lose his stride while following his father's footsteps down the sandy trails that lead to new places, discovery, and challenges. And every once in a while, this five-year-old boy will glance up at his father and say, "Daddy, is this the right way?" It's a simple request, a matter of trust. A sacred trust. And one that his daddy doesn't take lightly.

The loving care
we give our children
when they're young
is a reflection of
the unconditional love
they give us when we're old.

Chapter Ten

HAVE A GRATEFUL HEART

Louise Stark had quite a year back in 1989. That's when she met a fellow New Yorker named David, and they fell in love. Did she know he was "the one" when she met him? Absolutely.

"I knew in an instant. Actually, I think David knew, too, but it took him a year and a half to admit it."

David and Louise are professional people with good jobs. They are in their mid-thirties and they own two homes between them. Still, they longed for a new home to decorate together and, someday, they wanted to have a child. So why did they wait four years to plan their wedding day?

"It seems like we waited forever, but it was the right choice." In November 1989, Louise's mother, Anne, had a stroke and was also diagnosed with diabetes and arterial disease. It may be commonplace to hear of a woman in her late sixties having a stroke, but to her family, it was devastating news.

"David and I put *everything* on hold. Mom's health was the only thing that mattered, the only thing we could think about."

Caring for an aging parent is a major life change, and Louise wasn't prepared to think about it quite so soon. "My mom lived alone, and she was three hundred miles away. After Mom's stroke, I was making the five-hour drive to her house and back every other weekend. It just about killed me to have to leave her on Sunday."

Louise's father died in 1975. Her two sisters and her only brother also lived out of town. Louise felt that there really was no one to stay with her mother, so she continued to make weekend trips to check on Anne's health.

"My mom was not the type to ever tell me if something was wrong. I wasn't comfortable just calling her. I had to see her for myself."

The risk of Louise's mother having a second stroke was always in the back of her daughter's mind. "It scared me half to death when I thought about her being alone and so far away. I couldn't be there in less than five hours! The doctors were also concerned that she may not be taking her medication or eating right. Finally, I just told her one day that if she didn't come home with me, *I'd* be the next one having a stroke."

Naturally, Anne resisted. Like most people, she was quite proud of her independence. Louise's mother enjoyed living alone, coming and going as she pleased, and eating whenever she felt like it. Her privacy was very important to her, and she preferred living in the town where she had spent much of her life.

"Mom raised all four of us children in that house. She lived almost all of her thirty years of marriage there. Other than a large garden, which demanded her constant attention, all she had left was that house and her memories. She just didn't want to move and leave it all behind—not for me or anybody. There was nothing I could do to make her leave. So one day I told her, 'Mom, when you're ready, just tell me and I'll welcome you with open arms.' Meanwhile, I nearly went crazy while worrying about her constantly."

About six months passed before Anne realized her daughter's idea might make the best of a bad situation. Anne found it was becoming increasingly difficult to walk, and she tired easily. She grew lonely and her new physical challenges frightened her.

"During one of my visits, Mom looked at me with those big puppy dog eyes of hers and said, 'Louise, I think I'm ready now.' I was *so* relieved to hear her say that. We both knew that her move was inevitable, but she had to do it on her own schedule."

What Anne didn't know, however, was that David had just asked Louise to marry him. Now, his fiancee's mother was moving in with her. "Of course David was disappointed but he said that he was still committed to me. The timing was bad, but we both knew what we had to do. We put our marriage on hold indefinitely. Our families are important to us. They can never be replaced. David didn't need any explanation from me to understand.

"Mom sacrificed her whole life for us kids. I remember that when our dad died, it felt like we were burying a part of our mom along with him. She was only fifty-three when he passed away, and he was such a big part of her life. Off and on over the next ten years, I often walked in the house and found her all bundled up in her robe. She sat and stared, rocking back and forth in a chair for hours. That wasn't like my mom. She became extremely depressed. Even with all of us living in the area, she missed our dad terribly. Slowly, her old self returned as she grew more involved with us again. I didn't want her to ever feel that depressed or lonely. So, after her stroke, I wanted her with me and to be a part of my everyday life."

Louise and David put their plans on hold for four years while Anne adjusted to a new life with her daughter. "Our first year or so together was miserable. Mom hated living in the city, and she was afraid of always getting lost. She would drive only to the grocery store, and that made things even worse. I think she felt like she was living inside a prison. We both resented our loss of independence a little bit. Sometimes I felt like an overbearing, overprotective mother hen, but this was all so new to me. It was like I had suddenly become the parent and Mom was now the rebellious teenager. Things grew worse when she learned that David had proposed to me. She began to see herself as a burden to us, and she felt she was interfering in our lives. It was just awful.

"The whole time, I kept remembering what a great mother she was to me. I was the most independent child in our family, and Mom was very patient with me. She told me one day that while Dad was dying, he always asked her where his children were and what were we doing. From that day on, I never wanted Mom to wonder about what I was up to or where I had been. I was only sixteen, but she trusted me and I didn't want to let her down. So, I thought, now I'm thirty-six years old and it's my turn to be patient. David and I didn't know how long it would be before Mom got back on her feet and felt confident again. But, however long it took, we agreed to be there for her and be patient with her and with each other."

David's own mother had a five-bypass surgery performed in 1992. He's very close to his family, and Louise thinks his mother's experience helped him to understand the needs in her family, too. The time that Louise and Anne have spent together has also helped Anne get to know her future son-in-law very well. Likewise, David now regards Anne as his second mother.

Gradually over the last several years, Anne has made a good recovery. She's stronger now, and Louise says that her mother's confidence has returned. Anne no longer stays home all the time and she wants to get back into gardening. The return of Anne's complete independence has always been a goal shared by both Anne *and* Louise. When Louise first suggested that Anne visit a retirement apartment villa, Anne declared, "Please don't send me there to die!"

"You're not gonna die, Ma! You'll love it there! They have 400 tenants who are all about your own age. They organize field trips and offer aerobics, crafts, and classes … you won't ever have time to get bored."

Eventually, Anne visited the retirement community. Much to her surprise, there was no checking in or out unless she planned on being gone overnight. She also liked the idea of moving in all her own furniture into her new apartment. She could decorate it her own way. It was beginning to sound like fun. She checked out a few of the neighboring tenants and realized that they all had their own challenging circumstances, like she did. Furthermore, Anne realized that she missed being around people her own age, the school girl chats, and the afternoon lunches.

On her most recent visit to the complex, Anne overheard one resident asking another if she wanted to join her for a mile walk. The friend responded, "Definitely not. I don't believe in doing anything that's good for me."

"Oh, I'm gonna like *her*," Anne told Louise.

Louise's mother began to look forward to moving into her new apartment, with 400 new friends living nearby. David and Louise were married on December 26, 1993, and the couple moved into their own new home, filled to the ceiling with their hopes and dreams. It's time to move on for everyone, it seems.

"My mom always took such good care of me while I was growing up. Taking care of her for these past four years hardly compares to the sacrifices she's made for me over the course of my life. If I can help care for or assist Mom half as well or as often as she's cared for me, then I'll die a happy woman.

"When I left home, my mom said she'd be there for me if I ever needed her. That's how I want her to feel today. I *want* to be there for her. She's the person who taught me how to love unconditionally. Now she's stuck with me!"

The month before Anne was scheduled to move into her new apartment complex, she underwent major surgery. "The timing could not have been worse. Mom had her aorta replaced, her right kidney removed and bypass surgeries to her femoral arteries to improve the circulation in her legs. Forty-one days later, she and I were unpacking boxes of dishes and arranging her new kitchen. That's my mom! She's absolutely amazing!"

Louise told her mom that she expected Anne to visit her and David *every day* because they were only ten minutes away. "In fact," Louise said, "David had an extra house key made up for you. Plus, there's plenty of room for your garden out back."

Anne looked up from her box of dishes and gave her daughter a girlish grin. "Don't count on it, Louise."

Resentment is the acid that drips on our souls.

—Richard Speight

Chapter Eleven

LEARNING TO FORGIVE

"I was the oldest of eight children. I should have set an example. Instead, I walked out. I left and I never looked back." Carlos Martinez left home the day after he graduated from high school. His friends questioned why he waited so long.

Carlos Raul Martinez is the son of immigrant farm workers. His parents came to the United States so their children could get a good education and an opportunity to live better lives. His parents' aspirations for their children were not unlike those of most parents today. Even so, life was hard, and from the time they were infants, the Martinez children came to work with their parents in the fields. School was an exciting opportunity for all the Martinez children, if for no other reason than the time off it gave them from working since toddlers alongside their parents.

"The bright side of having to work so early in life was that we were with Mama and Papa all day, every day, until we started grade school. Our family was very close. We also developed a strong work ethic and a sense of pride in our work at an early age. It gave us self-esteem to be able to contribute in our family's daily routine.

"I don't know why my father started drinking like he did. Maybe because for the first time in his life he had some money to spend. Maybe it was the strain of working in the fields all his life. I don't know. I do remember Papa being bothered by the pesticides. Some days he would become so nauseated that he couldn't work the next day. His eyes bothered him, too. I remember how he was always rinsing his eyes out.

"Whatever the reason, Papa began drinking when I was twelve or thirteen years old. I avoided him when he got drunk. We all did. He would turn into a monster, accusing Mama of stealing his money or ridiculing me for eating more than my share. My younger sister and brothers would sometimes hide from him under our bed. We were afraid of our own father when he drank. The more he drank, the more we avoided him. The more we avoided him, the more distant our relationship grew. He became a stranger to us."

Carlos was the first in his family to graduate from high school. "I think the reason I was a good student was that school was a refuge for me. It was a place to go and take my mind off the problems of our family. I would sit in class and dream of becoming somebody else in a place far away. My studies were my escape route. In a sense, the more books I read, the more places I would visit. I liked to read and to learn. Learning opened possibilities for me. It opened my mind. I suppose I could have escaped using drugs just as easily, except that I knew if I turned to drugs, it would only add to my mother's pain. I also had an interested counselor in high school who encouraged me. He said that if I did well in school, I could go to college on a scholarship. When you're fifteen years old and somebody promises you a free ticket out, you'll do anything to get it. I chose learning."

Carlos graduated fifth in his class and received a full scholarship to college.

He went on to earn his master's degree in Business Administration from Texas A & M. After college, Carlos started his own family farming business, free from the use of any pesticides. His father left his mother the day Carlos graduated from high school. Mr. Martinez never knew of his son's achievements. No one was overly concerned to see the man leave, however, not even Carlos' mother.

"I imagine our mama was frightened by the thought of single parenting more than the fact that Papa was gone. I suppose she missed him. They were married for twenty-four years. I really don't know, but she may have been more relieved to see him go than she was sad. Anyway, I promised her I'd take care of her. She deserved to be taken care of. I worked while going to college and sent her money from every paycheck. It helped.

"One thing I do know is that I hated my father. I hated him all those years, and for what? I didn't know if he was alive or dead, and I didn't care.

"By the time I turned thirty-eight, I heard that Papa was not only alive, but he had stopped drinking entirely. He had actually been sober for the past five years." But that wasn't the only news Carlos learned regarding his father.

Mr. Martinez walked out of his home and the lives of his family without any explanation after attending Carlos' high school graduation ceremony in June 1973. Fifteen years past before Carlos heard that a stranger had called and told his brother that their father was dying from cancer. Still, no one really wanted to see him.

As the oldest brother, Carlos decided it was his obligation to go to his father's side. He said he did it for his mother. He said that *someone* had to do it. And later, Carlos said that he was glad he did.

"I was expecting to find a worn-out drunk. Instead, I discovered a man I barely knew, a man that I eventually came to admire."

When Carlos entered the small rented bungalow, he found a thin and fragile-looking old man who had lost most of his hair along with his angry attitude. "I would never have recognized him. The powerful, giant of a man I remembered as six feet tall had shrunk in size, stature, and spirit. He weighed less than one hundred pounds. The little hair he had left was entirely white. His face was pale, his cheeks full of rough grey stubble, and his eyes were sunken. He was a stranger to me once again.

"Papa was sitting in a chair, all wrapped up in a blanket, and staring without expression toward a small window. I was speechless and unsure if he really was our papa. He looked at me and said, 'Carlos, my son, what happened to you? You're fat.' Then I knew it was him. We laughed." One week later, Carlos buried his father and friend, along with many, many memories.

"We could have been friends sooner, but I waited too long. We became friends the week before he died. I wish that I had known him longer. I would have liked him. And I think he would have liked me, too."

The seven days Carlos spent with his father before he died were seven days that Carlos will never forget. The month was October, the year 1987. The leaves were off the trees and blowing. The nights were cold. They watched the World Series together on a dusty old black and white TV and they pretended nothing was wrong. They grew to like each other as if they had just met, as if they would be friends forever.

Carlos helped his father go to the toilet. He washed his bed sheets. He helped him eat what little he could, and he helped him again when his father threw up. He shaved his father's face and cut his hair. And when his father asked for his oldest son's forgiveness, Carlos forgave him. That evening, Carlos prayed that his father would suffer no longer. The following morning, Carlos' prayers were answered. Then the oldest son of a proud and humbled man laid him to rest.

"My father paid for his drinking and the sorrow he inflicted upon our mama a long time ago. He went to jail, and we never knew it. He had surgeries and chemotherapy, and we never knew it. He recovered from his addiction, and no one was there to congratulate him. Then he learned he was going to die, and no one was there to comfort him. That's a terrible price to pay for anyone. I would have forgiven him sooner if I had only known him."

Carlos had a lot of schooling, and his mother provided him with many examples of model behavior. But of all the lessons Carlos learned in life, perhaps the most powerful lesson of all was taught from the bedside of a broken man attempting to regain his respect as a father.

Over six years have passed since Carlos buried his father. He reluctantly admits that he is a smarter person now than he was in his younger years. "I only asked for a fifty/fifty relationship with my father. Now I realize that it should have been one hundred/one hundred. Fifty/fifty wasn't good enough.

"I must forgive myself, although I may not deserve to be forgiven. It is important to set my spirit free from the bondage of regret. By forgiving myself, I will help heal the hurt inside my own heart. My bitterness for my father ruined my soul. I can't change the past, but I will change the future. I must learn to forgive myself, to live without the pain, and become the son he would have been proudest to know."

Once
in a big blue moon
there comes a child
like your own.

Chapter Twelve

FAMILY PRIDE—
CELEBRATING OUR DIFFERENCES

"Families like ours are a dime a dozen. There's nothing spectacular about us."
Perhaps that's what I like most about Stan and Ann. They consider themselves
a typical, "average" couple, just like their parents.

Stan is a thirty-six-year-old African-American man whose family's roots were in farming in rural North Carolina. His father picked cotton to make a living before he joined the Navy. After serving his country, Stan's dad was the first in his family to graduate with a four-year college degree. His mother's family owned and operated a successful dairy farm. Stan's mother and father met in Statesville, North Carolina, where his mother earned her college degree. As early as 1955, when Stan's parents married, education was a priority in his family.

"Everybody wants their children to have opportunities they didn't have. My parents were no different in 1955 than we are today. Education is the key to closed doors."

Religion was also a strong part of Stan's family life. His parents raised him and his two younger sisters in the "Church of Christ tradition." It came as no surprise to Stan when his parents reacted favorably to the news of his wedding plans in 1986. Stan had known his wife for seven years before they married. He says his parents were grateful they chose to marry rather than "live in sin forever." It was a "typical" reaction from his church-going parents.

Stan is married to Ann, his wife of seven years. Ann is a thirty-three-year-old Caucasian woman. She was also raised by two hardworking and concerned parents. Her mother is a school teacher and her father worked for the same frozen food company most his life before retiring. Like Stan's folks, Ann's parents also earned college degrees, and they place a high value on their education. And like Stan's mom and dad, Ann's parents also have always wanted what's best for their daughter and her two younger brothers.

Ann's father served in the Air Force National Guard and earned the highest enlisted rank before his retirement. He left the military after thirty-two years of service and was the State Senior Enlisted Advisor for the State of Virginia. Naturally, Ann's father ran a tight ship while watching his three children grow up. There was no room for laziness or disrespect in this Virginia household. Ann's father was proud when she graduated as an "A" student from public high school in Charlottesville. It didn't surprise Ann's father that his daughter was smart. Nor did it surprise Ann's mother that her daughter was dating the high school's track star. What did surprise Ann's parents, however, was that their daughter chose to date a young black man.

It was even more surprising to Ann's parents when she dropped the track star to go out with Stan, whom she met in college. "You're asking for problems," Ann's mother warned. "Life is hard enough without inviting racial difficulties."

Her parents' reservations had nothing to do with Stan as a person. They wanted their only daughter and subsequent grandchildren to have a life without hardship, a life filled with opportunities and prosperity. It was not unlike what Stan's parents wanted for their *only* son and grandchildren. It was a typical reaction from "average" middle American parents.

When the news of Stan and Ann's wedding plans reached Ann's relatives, her mother anticipated the family would "disown" Ann. Nevertheless, Ann married Stan on August 9, 1986.

"I expected less than a warm reception," said Stan. But this time it was Stan who got surprised.

"Why shouldn't they like Stan?" said Ann. "He's terrific! He's a great guy, and I knew my family would see that eventually."

Ann's grandmother was eighty-eight years old. She lived through two world wars and the Korean War. She knew firsthand the senselessness of prejudice. Once her respected words of wisdom were heard, the rest of Ann's relatives joined in and welcomed Stan into their family with open arms. It wasn't immediate, and it wasn't a simple act. But it was a necessary act that began with the pale outstretched arms of a strong and insightful grandmother.

Not unlike their parents, Stan and Ann were driven by the need to better themselves and to provide greater opportunities for their future children. With college degrees in hand and their suitcases full of parental high hopes and best wishes, Ann and Stan relocated to the Washington, D. C. area and began a new life together.

Five years later, the first grandchild for both families was born. "Stan has always been totally supportive of my dreams and ambitions. He was no different throughout my pregnancy and in the delivery room. I think that's why things went as smoothly as they did." Their daughter's birth came after four and one half hours of labor. She was a "routine" delivery—routine for everyone other than her parents, that is. They named their daughter Savannah. And on an early morning in June, the three of them began an entirely new life together, but not without high hopes handed down through generations.

"Savannah is *very* pretty," said Ann. "She's breathtaking," interrupted her father. "She's *so* beautiful, we wonder if she may have it rough later in life."

Stan and Ann sound a lot like their own parents. They want only the very best for their little girl. In the summer of 1994, they will drop Savannah off at a private preschool, along with all their hopes and dreams for her future. Her parents don't worry about the color of her skin, but that their daughter's beauty and gender may become an obstacle for Savannah later in life. They worry that a beautiful woman may not always be taken seriously inside the business community.

"By entering Savannah in a Montessori preschool, we hope she'll start out a step ahead of the rest." Ann and Stan feel it is critical for their daughter to have an early start on her education. They pray that she'll become a smart and caring person, a business woman and compassionate leader, somebody strong that will endure and rise above life's inevitable hardships. Their prayers sound familiar.

There's one more aspect of life that Stan and Ann want their daughter to learn. As children, neither of them thought too much about their family heritage. Now that they are parents, that has changed. They want their daughter to learn from their own family histories. Stan and Ann feel that with knowledge comes understanding and a sense of pride, no matter what a person's skin color may be. In this respect, Savannah has a unique opportunity for learning that neither Stan, Ann, nor her grandparents had. Savannah has an intimate opportunity to learn about her country's history and her family heritage from two different perspectives and from the people who have lived them.

"We have family pictures everywhere, but I want Savannah to know as much about our personal family backgrounds as possible. My father, especially, has a lot to learn from," said Stan. "He has lived life full circle. He knows family stories from the days of slavery, and he's lived through the Civil Rights era. Some night I'm going to sit him down and let the tape recorder run. Just think how great it will be someday to have our grandchildren learn about history by hearing their great-grandfather speak."

Ann wants Savannah to know about her great-grandmother, a woman she has always admired. "She was my age once, and she had a two-year-old, just like we do. I want Savannah to know what it was like back then. My grandmother lived on the same farm for sixty years. I came across a picture of her taken on the farm that is really special to me. I have it still. Before my grandfather bought the farm, he worked there as a farmhand. My grandparents lived through so much history.

And being a farmer, my grandmother was a very strong woman. She's a wonderful role model for Savannah and me. Her farm was self-supportive for over one hundred years. That's something to be proud of, and something her great-granddaughter should know about."

Stan and Ann are witnesses to a different time in history than their parents or grandparents. Some things are better now, but some are not—each generation has its own challenges. But there are certain timeless qualities about the family that remain unchanged. Most parents want what is best for their children. Likewise, most parents want their children to know about their family heritage. This common bond does not change with skin color or the challenges of each new era. In these ways, Savannah's parents, grandparents, and ancestors are alike.

"Someday," said Stan, "I'll be an old man sitting in my father's armchair. I'll tell my grandchildren stories of their great-grandfather who used to pick cotton for a living when he was young before going off to war."

Savannah learns about her heritage every day, not only by listening, but by watching her parents, too. "The examples we give our daughter were taught to us by our parents," said Ann. "Our family histories are only part of the heritage we hope to pass on to Savannah. The other part, the unspoken words, are what really makes Savannah's heritage unique."

Stan and Ann are giving Savannah unique and sometimes difficult lessons, and their daughter will be a richer person for the experience. It's their blend of parental care and concern that makes celebration and family pride possible. Whether "average" or not, families like Stan and Ann's are worth far more than "a dime a dozen," especially since *love* is their primary currency.

Growing up happens in a heartbeat.
One morning you wake up, and you're no longer sharing
a bedroom with your older brother. He's moved away and
has kids of his own. Now, he's become someone else's hero.
But you can always look back on your memories.
Only when you look back do you come
to realize that life is about the Journey.

Chapter Thirteen

INSPIRATION AND YOUR GREATEST INFLUENCE

Gary William Lee was smarter than his younger sister, Janet. After all, he chose the side of their bedroom that had the door. Then he cleverly stretched out masking tape and stuck it down on the hardwood floor, thereby setting a precedent for the "Laws of the Bedroom."

"See there," he said to Janet. "This is my side and that's your side. I divided it equal, so shut your trap and stay clear of my side." Then he turned out the light and they went to sleep in their respective corners of the small bedroom.

"He's a pretty okay brother," Janet thought as she drifted off to sleep. "Now at least we won't have to fight anymore, and I'll live to see my ninth birthday."

Gary always made up the rules because he was the oldest and therefore, the wisest. Gary was *almost* thirteen, practically a grown-up. "He knew everything about anything," Janet claimed. "He even smoked an occasional cigarette back then." But he also said that if he ever caught his little sister smoking he'd kill her, so she never did. "Well, except for once," she added with a smile.

Continuing her story, Janet said it wasn't until the next morning that she discovered she would have to cross over Gary's line of tape in order to use the bathroom. She thought about jumping over it, but if she missed, Gary would wake up for sure. If he opened his eyes and found her on *his* side of the room, he'd have to kill her to keep his "Big Brother" status. There was only one thing Janet *could* do.

She glanced up at the classic blue closet-dresser that stood against the wall leading to the doorway. It was really tall, almost to the ceiling. If she pulled out the drawers, she could easily climb up to the top of the dresser and then crawl across it to the doorway. So, one at a time, Janet pulled out the drawers and climbed her way to the top. "Piece of cake," she thought.

"Won't Gary be surprised to wake up and see me gone!" she whispered under her breath. About this time, Janet felt the dresser slowly tilting forward with her weight. Everything came crashing down on top of her in a huge commotion that could have shaken the house. She woke up just about everyone with the noise, including their dog, Rocky, who barked steadily.

"The dresser was really heavy, but I was cushioned by stuffed socks and underwear. Gary and Mom lifted it off me. Clothes hangers were everywhere. I was a little bit scared. Mom was hysterical with concern, while Gary was hysterical with laughter. Dad was still snoring. A freight train couldn't wake *him* up."

Janet didn't tell her mother that Sunday morning back in 1963 just what had prompted her to climb up the dresser at 6:00 a.m.

"Get this mess cleaned up before your father wakes up—and what's that tape doing all over the floor? You kids have some serious cleaning up to do before church. Now, get going and I mean it," their mother scolded.

"Mom walked away with a heavy sigh," Janet remembered. "I didn't tell her anything." Janet saw no reason to get her brother in trouble, too. "After all," she said, "he was the oldest, the wisest, and no doubt, the *biggest* brother in the entire East Bay Area."

Growing up happens in a heartbeat. One morning you wake up, and you're no longer sharing a bedroom with your older brother. He's moved away and has kids of his own. Now, he's become someone else's hero. But you can always look back on your memories. Only when you look back do you come to realize that life is about the Journey. It's about everything that happens while your making those big plans.

Janet and Gary's father died recently. Most of their memories of him were good ones, although they had their share of bad ones, too. What they prefer to remember is up to them. Mostly, they've chosen to think about the good times and repeat them as much as possible with their own families.

Recalling her childhood, Janet spoke of many winters spent in their vacation mountain cabin. After a major snowstorm, her dad was the only means of transportation. He stood six foot three and never complained when he pulled his kids through waist-high snow on a toboggan packed full of groceries.

Janet especially remembered the time she got lost walking home in a blizzard. As she began to panic, growing more and more confused with her directions, Dad appeared out of the whiteness. He stood as tall as a redwood, and his strength calmed her fears as he carried her safely home on his back through the white-out.

Gary recalled the summer he turned fifteen and longed for a motorcycle. "We couldn't afford one, so Dad built one from scratch, just like he built our cabin. Dad could do anything … or at least he tried."

"That's true," said his sister. "He almost burned the place down, too! When he was gluing down plastic tiles on the bathroom walls, his pipe ignited the fumes and an explosive fire broke out. Mom and Dad rushed us outside. I remember sitting on the tree swing in our front yard, crying, while watching them fight the fire. We were on forestry land, miles from a fire station. But Mom and Dad put the fire out before it did anything more than destroy the bathroom. Luckily, no one got hurt very badly. Mom was relieved the fire was out, but she wasn't too happy with Dad.

"I remember lots of times when I was scared and Mom or Dad was always there to comfort me and make me feel safe again."

"*My* childhood was a little harder on our folks than yours," Gary said.

"Like the time you nearly cut off your foot with Dad's chain saw," Janet interrupted.

"I was cutting wood!" said her brother, defensively. "Our folks lived through that one pretty well. I guess I'm lucky my own kids aren't as dangerous as I was."

"And don't forget the time you climbed up that dead Jefferson pine out back and fell fifty or sixty feet to the ground. You barely missed a jagged stump, as I recall. I remember watching you dangling from a piece of loose bark like a rag doll before you fell. You were hollering for me to run and get Dad, and the fear in your voice terrified me. I thought you were invincible—until then. I returned with Mom and Dad only to find you lying on your back on a pile of dead wood. The wind was knocked out of you and huge tree branches were poking through one arm. You were a case and a half. I'm amazed that they decided to keep you around ... just kidding." She smiled up at her big brother.

"Looking back," Gary continued, "I now realize just how much they were a team and helped each other out during our younger years."

"And they never fainted at the sight of your blood either," said Janet.

Gary ignored his little sister. "We put them through a lot, but back then we had no idea of the pain we caused them. We could have been worse, naturally, but I guess we brought them a lot of joy, too. When you're a kid, you don't think about anything but yourself. It's really not until you have your own kids that you realize just how hard parenting is. We all make our own share of mistakes, and Mom and Dad were no exception. In spite of any mistakes made, they were still my greatest influence while growing up. It's only now that I'm forty-three years old and a parent, that I can appreciate all they did for me. I'd like to know I'm doing even half as well at parenting as Mom and Dad did."

"He's right," Janet said. "They were both really hard workers, too. In fact, Mom still works hard today at age seventy. She and Dad instilled a work ethic in us by their example, more than by their words. They cleared the land themselves and built our cabin together by hand. And when it was done, we had all chipped in somewhere and the place became a symbol of our family's love, sweat, and tears. That particular day of the fire, I learned a lot about fire hazards, but I learned even more about how much we meant to one another. I didn't want to lose our home, but I was more afraid of losing each other. Guess it's no wonder that I ended up a firefighter *and* a mom."

"We were lucky to have a lot of the things we did," Gary went on. "We weren't rich by any means. My first set of wheels was a made-from-scratch scooter we called the 'tote-goat,' and your first bike was a boy's bike, too big for you and full of scratches. But we were happy. We felt rich because we had both a mom and a dad who gave us their love and encouraged us to do our best in whatever we did. We knew they cared about us. Some kids grow up and never know that."

Janet and Gary's father was a precision machinist, and he placed a great deal of importance on practical knowledge, like construction, mechanics, and ecological responsibilities. Their mother was a grade school teacher. "Mom felt that the key to success was found in your desire to learn and in higher education," said Janet. "She encouraged us to work our way through college because she felt education was something we could fall back on. 'Learn as much as you can,' Mom would say, 'because you can never learn too much—and no matter what happens to you in life, no one can ever rob you of your knowledge.'

"We both have a little college in us, but what really made a difference in our lives was taught to us in our home and not in school. It was in the examples our parents gave us, and the everyday sacrifices they made for us. Mom finished her own college education by going to night school so she could become a teacher and have the summers free to be with us. Those summers were the best days of my childhood, and Mom made them possible. Parenthood is about sacrifice and giving. There is no such thing as a selfish parent, and we were fortunate enough to have two of them for as long as we did."

"My wife, Lana, and I have been married for fifteen years," said Gary, "but we were separated for two years in between. Now, when I get home from work, I light a fire in the fireplace and sit back and admire my family. We all take turns fixing dinner one night a week. No matter how the food tastes, when I look at our two gorgeous daughters, Rhonda and Jennifer, I'm reminded to count my blessings. I'm thankful that we're all together again. I do a lot of duck hunting and fishing. I'm not around every weekend like some fathers are, but I'm always happy to come home, and what's better, my family's always happy to see me. That's what it's all about."

Gary's eyes began to tear up and he stopped talking. I got a lump in my throat as I watched him. Gary's a big man, well over six feet tall. He probably weighs 250 pounds. When such a giant of a man becomes sentimental, his heart is reflected in his eyes. I could tell that Gary's heart was as big as he was.

"Gary's really mellowed in his old age," Janet said as she hugged her big brother. "Rumor has it that he bakes bread on occasions, and he's been known to fall asleep on the sofa with his daughters' cat curled up on his stomach. There was a day not too long ago when cats were absolutely unheard of in their house!" Gary said nothing in defense, so his sister continued talking, edging him on. "And he drove a pickup truck loaded with the neighborhood kids, all dressed up, standing in the back truck bed for the local Fourth of July parade down Main Street. I even heard from a *very* reliable source," she poked her brother's belly with her finger as she spoke, "that you're thinking of planting some roses in your front yard this Spring!" Finally, Gary had heard enough.

"Well, okay, you heard right. But Bonkers [the cat] is different! So, I'm mellowing out a little. The fact is that my family has made me younger, not older. I'm more proud of my girls than any fish I've ever caught. Having a family like mine to come home to makes everything else in life secondary compared to the way they make me feel."

"No doubt about that. If you ever want to see something special," said Janet, "you should see the look in his youngest daughter's eyes when she's with her dad. Jennifer is thirteen and without a doubt, she is certified 'nuts' about Gary. She even wears his old flannel shirts to school." Janet looked up at her brother and said, "Who would have thought your old crap would ever become a fashion statement?" she laughed. "I guess she's just as crazy about you as I was at her age … and then some. Mom told me that you even taught Jenn how to ride her bike when she was younger, just like you taught me. Isn't it great to know that you can still be someone's hero when you're such an old fart?

"Gary made a great impression on me when I was a kid. No doubt about it, I was his biggest fan. But now that I'm supposedly all grown up, I look back and realize that it was our folks who made the greatest impression on me. I just never knew it until now. Everybody has a parent. But there are parents ... and then there are parents. No matter what we had or didn't have while growing up, or what our parents shortcomings may have been, we still knew all along that we were loved. Mom and Dad made a positive difference in our lives. What more can you ask of a parent than that?

"I'll always remember the good times we shared and being together as a family. Now that I'm a parent, I try to let our son know that he's loved. I try to make happy memories for him to remember and cherish, too."

Just then, Janet's three year old came running out onto the patio shouting, "I'm all done, Mama! I'm all done with my nap now! And it took a long time! Shall we go have ice cream, shall we?"

The boy's mother smiled down at him and said, "Going for ice cream cones at Moo's Ice Cream across from Nichol Park was a Sunday family tradition in our youth. Great idea—let's go! Uncle Gary can drive."

Janet got up slowly, still thinking, and added, "Our parents did a great job raising Gary and me, and it wasn't easy. It's never easy. Parenting is not a job for everyone. But for those who choose it, the lessons learned from their childhood and passed along to their own children have an incredible impact on us all."

"I think a good parent becomes everyone's hero, in a sense," said Gary. "Heroes don't have to be Olympic gold medalists or highly paid basketball stars or even your big brother. Sometimes they're just moms and dads."

Change we did not seek
but now embrace
This privilege to continue
in life's race.

—Dan Kirkbride

Chapter Fourteen

LETTING GO

One year after a Wyoming rancher named Dan Kirkbride met his new wife, Lynn, he wrote down some thoughts on a yellow legal pad. He was thinking about a special day that took place six years ago in 1987:

Looking back in my Day-Timer, I see that we branded the heifers' calves on June 2, 1987. At the time it seemed like a routine day on the job, but it has since taken on great significance. That morning was the only time I ever met a man who was to become one of the most important people in my life.

Almost every good branding includes a guest or two. Our visitor that morning was a young pastor named Chuck. He came with my brother's pastor, an annual helper on this particular project. Both men contributed as full participants. Cows bawled. Fence posts smoked. Fathers coached their kids. Horse sweat, manure and blue sky blended in a ritual decades old.

We finished by noon and went back to my brother's for lunch. Did Chuck mention his recent move from Chicago or how well he liked it in the West? Did he talk about his wife and two small boys? Frankly, I don't remember. We all went our separate ways after lunch, and I never saw Chuck again.

Five years later the scene shifts to a bereavement support group in a hospital basement. There, a collection of elderly ladies and I have gathered to consider the loss of our spouses. It's our last meeting celebrated by a potluck dinner. Into the room swishes an attractive, thirty-something woman wearing purple and toting a pan of cream puffs. She looks out of place in this setting and I conclude she has walked into the wrong meeting.

But it's okay. She, too, had lost her spouse the previous year. She mentions that he was a minister—a minister named Chuck. Before the evening ends, I make a dim connection.

"You know, I think I met your husband once," I say to the cream puff lady. "He came and helped us brand." Later conversations confirm the details. In fact, she said that Chuck had been thrilled by the day on the range, and he even called his folks in Milwaukee to tell them all about it.

But he could never have imagined the full importance of that trip to the country. He could not have guessed that his lovely wife would some day go on in life with the man on the brown horse. And he would not have envisioned his boys as heirs to that pen of crossbred calves.

And so wrote forty-year-old "Cowboy Dan the Man," as he was called, a hard-working rancher who dearly loved his wife and two daughters, a man who never asked for any changes in his life, a man who accepted his fate and wanted only what was best for his girls. Cowboy Dan slugged it out, grieved his losses, praised his blessings, and eventually fell in love all over again with the cream puff lady dressed in purple.

Dan's first wife, Pam, was diagnosed with breast cancer during the summer of 1988. She fought the cancer with all her strength, but lost the battle in December 1991. "The detection was early, but Pam was one of a small percent for whom the treatments failed." When she died, their two girls were six and nine years of age. Pam and Dan had been married just about eighteen years. It's not a parting that most married people can imagine coping with. In time, however, Dan realized that the best he could do was keep her memory alive in spirit and continue living his life with gladness, as impossible as that seemed.

Dan had mourned his wife's illness and passing the entire three and one-half years she was sick. There were mornings too numerous to mention where he struggled with his emotions. After a considerable grieving time, Dan urged himself to consider what tomorrow would bring for his girls and for him. And with the future in mind, he managed to spend less time looking at his past.

He retained a housekeeper for the chores and cooking, but Dan nurtured the girls himself, and he did it with gusto. Dan recognized that they, too, had a grieving process to endure. What little energy he had left was consumed by his 13,000-acre ranch and approximately 1,300 head of cattle. At one point, Dan constructed a half-mile-long fence on his property requiring nearly three thousand heavy blows with a post pounder. He didn't feel ready to take on the reconstruction of his own life until he was done with the fence. Soon afterward, Dan attended a local grief support group meeting, with consequences that changed his family's life forever.

Lynn Westerman grew up in Milwaukee where she met and married Chuck before relocating to Chicago in 1979. She had never been on a ranch before. In fact, Lynn had never even known a farmer when she and Chuck decided to move their family from Chicago's inner city to Wyoming's high plains. Chuck was eager to begin his new position as pastor for an American Baptist church in Cheyenne. Young, hopeful and bright, Chuck had brought new life to the church by the time he was diagnosed with cancer in June 1990. When the news hit, Lynn and Chuck had been married almost eleven years and they had three young boys, ranging in age from three months to seven years.

Lynn handled her husband's illness with courage, grace, and honesty. She asked that her family and friends do the same, and they responded with open enthusiasm. When he died in May 1991, Lynn urged friends to say their goodbyes to Chuck and carry on, always remembering his life's work and words of inspiration. "Death does not carry the final word," she advised them. "Chuck lives inside every one of us as long as we remember him."

Their congregation and friends continued to support Lynn and her three boys long after Chuck's funeral. Many of them cooked Lynn's family meals, and everyone helped when it came time for her and the boys to move into a rented home. Because of their support, as well as her keeping a journal and using outside counseling, Lynn didn't "crash and burn." Instead, she rose to the occasion and continued her caring role as mother and friend to her children in the long months following her husband's death. Like Dan, Lynn also realized that her boys would need much time and nurturing to adjust to life's changes. "The kids have done better than I could have hoped, but it's been no small deal for them, either." Approximately sixteen months later, Lynn accepted a new job in rehab for Goodwill Industries, trying her best to get on with life.

"During Chuck's illness, I was especially grateful that the Lord gave me a young baby to care for along with our other two boys. Breastfeeding little Charlie was great therapy for me. It was a natural source of healing to be able to touch and hold him, and to love and hold onto Jeremy and Mick. They gave me the strength I needed to carry on. I couldn't imagine going through such a change without them.

"About six months after Chuck's death was when it really hit me. On top of everything else, it was hard to be single and a mother of three at age thirty-six. I didn't know what the ground rules were. I had no idea how to get on with my life as far as ever dating again. I knew I was vulnerable though, so I chose my company wisely. Then I went out and bought an entire new wardrobe. That helped me feel good again, and I felt a little closer to starting my life over. By the time I met Dan at the support meeting, I was ready to try dating. I was anxious to swap stories and get to know him better, but I didn't know where to start."

Lucky for Lynn, Dan did. Two months after meeting Lynn, he wrote her a four-page letter. She responded and soon after, they had their first date. They went to dinner and afterwards, sat out on Lynn's porch and talked until midnight. It was a balmy August night, conducive to talking, although they didn't need much persuasion.

Lynn didn't only fall head-over-heels in love with Dan. She also liked Dan's girls. "Abby and Hannah were their names, and they were as beautiful as you could imagine! I liked them from the start. All the kids were enthusiastic about the possibilities as they became acquainted with each other. They are all relatively close in age and have since grown to genuinely care for each other. God really had His hand on this whole thing. It isn't just Dan and I who are happy. *All* of us are."

The children and their parents spent much time together in the weeks that followed introductions. They took in a few Rockies' games and went to a circus in Denver. At the ranch, they piled onto a trailer hitched to Dan's all-terrain-vehicle and had picnics out on the range. Everyone was thrilled, including their relatives. It didn't take long before Dan and Lynn knew that everything was going to work out fine.

"It was a *great* match without compromises for any of us," said Lynn. "Of course, trying to accomodate the needs of five children will always be a challenge. And the kids, especially the girls, had to give up a lot in terms of their space and privacy. Abby and Hannah went from a quiet house and single rooms to intermittent bedlam and having to share with three brothers. The boys also had their share of sacrifices to make. They moved from their familiar school, sports activities, and church to a new environment forty miles away. There were adjustments for everyone, but we were all willing and optimistic at the same time." The only ones who weren't enthusiastic were Lynn's old dog and Dan's family cat.

Dan and Lynn were married on April 18, 1993. Flowers were placed in the church foyer in memory of Pam Kirkbride and Charles Westerman. Together, along with 400 friends and family, Dan and Lynn acknowledged both families' past and celebrated their new future as one.

Today, they continue to keep the memory of their children's deceased parents alive. "Their existence is never denied," said Lynn. "When their names are brought up, we continue to talk openly about the other life our kids once knew. Dan and I believe that parents set the tone. We have as much to remember from our past as we have to celebrate today for our new future. The kids are thriving in this environment. Discussing their feelings openly is the key."

"Of everybody involved," said Dan, "it's probably the hardest on their grandparents, both Pam and Chuck's parents. Coping is more difficult for each of them because they grieve the loss of their children every day. For them, there is no replacement for love lost. For them, the pain is neverending, which makes it really hard to let go. Ultimately, however, they want what's best for their grandchildren, as do we. They try their best, taking it one day at a time, which is all anyone can ever do.

"For a long time, Lynn and I had to slug it out by ourselves. Believe me, until we met each other, there was a lot of 'slugging' going on. But we fulfilled our contracts with our spouses, and they sent us forward in life with their blessings. Lynn and I each did our own grief homework following the deaths. Since then, we have felt no constraints to look back. The grieving process is never easy, but it's always necessary. We both knew that."

Six months after their marriage, Dan had all the cowpokes any rancher would ever need. Young Mick and Abby, who are seven and eight, routinely help their dad check on the windmills. The older children, Jeremy and Hannah, drove 242 steers alongside their father on horseback last fall.

"And earlier this summer," said Dan, "when it came time to release the 900-pound steers from their trailer, I turned to one of my partners and said, 'Here's a good job for you, Charlie.'

"So three-year-old Charlie climbed up on the fender and began fumbling with the latch. He finally pulled the pin out triumphantly, but he couldn't get the handle free of the chain while the cattle nervously stomped inside. It probably took Charlie two whole minutes to find the combination, but eventually the handle gave way, the gate swung open, and the steers bolted to freedom.

"It was Charlie's first summer on the job. For the most part, he's one of the better hired men in this county," his dad said, with a smile in his voice. "Charlie and his four older siblings may have slowed me down some while working on the ranch this year, but they've taught me a lot, too. We're all students of life. You can teach your kids daily tasks, but attitudes just come along for the ride. No matter if you're raising Charlie's or Charlotte's, your kids are still your most important crops."

And lately, Dan has had the best crop ever. He helps raise their five children as a team—everyone chips in and they all have a voice. He's also their basketball and flag football coach, and he heads the 4-H Club's livestock project the kids have enrolled in. Having a dad to tell ten-year-old Jeremy "what I'm not doing right" in sports is a small part of the many blessings Dan has brought to Lynn and the boys.

"I had a great guy the first time around," Lynn said, "but to have a second husband and father for the boys equally good as the first is nothing short of a miracle in my book! The girls also have added another dimension to our lives that the boys and I never dreamed possible. When it's right, you simply know it, and life is too short to waste.

"I held a promise of Scripture very close to my heart the year after Chuck died. In Jeremiah it reads, 'For I know the plans I have for you, declares the Lord . . . plans to prosper you and not to harm you, plans to give you hope and a future. I will be found by you and will bring you back from captivity.'

"People *can* start over, although at the time, it may seem too much to ask of us. Like Dan, I had my children to think about first. Now, they too, are blessed with a new beginning. Nothing in this world could compare to the happiness I know in my life today. That's not to say that I am larger than life or that the road hasn't been hard. It's been *real* hard. The only larger-than-life aspects of our story is the help from our friends and family and God's goodness, too, in letting Dan and me find each other."

Dan added, "Recovering from the death of a loved one is never easy, and it's important that you don't become discouraged by the process. It takes time to heal and you must allow for it. Lynn and I both have so many friends and family, including our children, to thank for pulling us through. Occasionally, I need to remind myself that it's the people, not the cows, which really count in life. And our kids remind me every day that life isn't filled with useless clutter. Things matter. Nothing is ever wasted."

Two months after Dan's marriage to Lynn, he sat at his desk and wrote the following:

> Someone once said that it's as if we're on the underside of a great tapestry in life and the pattern above us looks random and confusing. But one day, we'll look out and view the tapestry from above and we'll find that everything makes sense. We'll see that God has crafted a masterpiece with every stitch in place.

This is the tapestry that Dan, Lynn, and their five children are a part of today. They have grieved their losses and have given praise each day for their many blessings. Most of all, they have learned to embrace the privilege to continue in life's race.

*Just think how great
the world would be
if all our children saw
was Good.*

Chapter Fifteen

MAKING THE WORLD A BETTER PLACE

Julianne Hannaford was a food server at a popular restaurant for four years. Everyone enjoyed her company, including her customers. Anyone who has ever waited tables will tell you that the work is extremely hard. Julianne was one of those great waitresses who always managed a smile even when her body ached.

"Keeping your customers happy is only part of it. The other part is demanding of your muscle strength. It's very strenuous. Food trays are heavy. Pitchers of water are heavy. There's a lot of lifting, stooping, and bending. It's not a job for everyone."

Julianne wasn't totally in love with her job. Like many, she worked because she and her husband, Jim, had no choice financially. She was reluctant to give up the money just because she was feeling tired and her body hurt. Julianne has never been a quitter.

But as the months passed, she found her job was physically becoming harder and harder to take. She thought to herself that at thirty years of age, she was a little too young to be feeling so old. Then one evening after her shift, Julianne's legs began to cramp up on her. On the way home, she had to pull over because she couldn't manage her car's brake and accelerator pedals. After a few minutes massaging her legs, Julianne's muscles began to relax and she continued on her way.

But when her weakness became noticeable on the job, her employer cut her work load from four tables to three and limited her duties. That was a little hard for Julianne to accept. She had always been a hard worker, and she felt badly not being able to carry her fair share.

Julianne reflected on her own childhood one afternoon while playing with her daughter. She had always thought she would grow up to be a homemaker much like her mother. Most of all, Julianne remembered those times she spent alone with her mother and how much they meant to her.

"I have a special relationship with my mom. We're real friends. I looked forward to having unlimited time together and that special bond with my own daughter someday." Julianne's family took lots of summer trips to Hot Springs, Arkansas while she was growing up. That's where she and her three brothers learned to swim, dive and, most of all, water ski. They were happy times that she looked forward to repeating as a parent.

Now, Julianne wondered fleetingly if she was creating her aches and pains in her mind. Her childhood dream had always been to stay home and raise her daughter, rather than working outside the home. As ridiculous as it seemed, perhaps it *was* all in her head. "What else could be causing such fatigue?" she thought.

By the time their daughter turned four years old, Julianne and Jim had learned that Julianne's fatigue and muscle pain was not all in her head after all. Julianne was diagnosed with a debilitating disorder thought to be genetic, myotonic muscular dystrophy. She was thirty-one.

"I was finally diagnosed the day before our daughter's fourth birthday. It made me even more determined to give Elise the best 'Circus Birthday Party' she could ever imagine. My awful visit to the doctor's office wasn't going to ruin *her* day!"

Julianne continued working, not really knowing what her time frame would be for the inevitable cane or wheelchair. Again, working wasn't a matter of choice. Julianne had no health insurance and her nine months of diagnostic testing were financially devastating.

"At first, everyone was in shock with my diagnosis, including me. We didn't know that muscular dystrophy could happen in adults. Nor did we have any prior family history of it. We all had trouble accepting the news.

"My momma and daddy cried rivers, wishing they could change it or do something to make it all better. They suggested I contact the Muscular Dystrophy Association for assistance. MDA was a big help in answering our endless questions and reassuring us that they would be there whenever I needed them. My husband became very protective in a way that seemed foreign to me. Jim worried too much. They *all* worried too much!

"My work load wasn't as heavy as it had been. However, I was still having a hard time doing a good job, and the pain was incredibly hard to take. I remember picking up our daughter from preschool one afternoon after my shift ended. I was sore and my legs were cramping up so badly that by the time we got home, I couldn't get out of the car. I let Elise out of her car seat and then laid myself across the front seat for thirty minutes. Elise was only four and she played in the car as if she understood my pain completely. Like always, she was an angel.

"Eventually, I managed to get out of the car and crawl into the house with Elise at my side. I had always felt a strong bond with her, but now she knew a part of me that drew us even closer together. She was curious, yet tender.

"I got up on the couch and laid there and just cried. Elise came over to me, unprompted, and began rubbing my legs. She kissed my tears and patted my face and then she told me that everything was going to be all right. Elise was so strong and compassionate. I'll never forget that special moment. It was as if I were the child and Elise, the comforting voice and touch of Momma."

Julianne collapsed one more time before quitting her job. She was physically unable to work after that. The experience caused her to lay flat on her back for almost three weeks. This time, Jim was there to see his wife crumble and fall. Having known her prior lifestyle, it was frightening enough for him to insist that they didn't need the money as much as they needed Julianne. Clearly, her body was ready for retirement even if her mind didn't necessarily agree.

Julianne thought about a lot of things as she lay bedridden for several weeks. She reflected on her strong family ties and the heartache and concern her health was causing everyone. She thought about how helpless they all were, wanting to change things, yet powerless to do so. So much agony was spent in vain. She also thought about never being able to water ski again and how she would miss it. She got teary eyed thinking that Elise would never know the person her mother once was—the active, competitive athlete inside her. Julianne felt alone, although she was grateful for having done these active things in the first place. Still, she thought about all the things she wanted to do, yet couldn't. No one really understood what she was going through. How could they?

"No matter how strong my family ties were, this was one struggle that no one could fight for me. I had to fight this one by myself, and I had to do it well because my daughter was watching. I prayed to God for courage, and I asked Him for guidance. He was the only one that I could talk to that really understood. God gave me peace and inner strength. He was my true comforter."

Then this tired wife and mother began counting her blessings more seriously. Now Julianne could stay home with her daughter, and the timing couldn't be any better! They'd have an entire year to spend together at home before Elise would begin school. "All the aches and pains in the world were worth that. My prayers had been answered."

Ultimately, Jim and Julianne felt lucky and blessed in spite of Julianne's muscular dystrophy. "Elise has always been a blessing to us. She's so special, so sensitive to others in need, and so giving of her love. There can't be another person on this earth as wonderful as Elise, and no one could be more grateful than us. And she's still so young! She's only a little person, but she has so much compassion and strength. There's so much yet to look forward to together. Elise will always be our miracle come true."

Julianne did a lot of soul-searching. She spoke to the Lord daily, and she said that His response was simple: "I am with you always."

"Don't worry about it," she thought. "Be happy and accept whatever God offers. Perhaps this is how I was suppose to be. It's God's plan. I decided to stop trying to control my life and just enjoy the ride. Knowing that I'm not alone in my struggle gives me the ability to cope with my progressive muscle weakness. And God doesn't allow a burden we can't handle. This became more evident every day for me. We all have thorns in our side of some sort. My problems are no greater than anyone else's. In fact, one year after I was diagnosed with MD, my youngest brother was also diagnosed with it.

"I don't focus on what I can't do, but I don't want to be judged merely on what I've had to overcome, either. I want to be judged on what I've *accomplished*. In spite of my disability, I'm still a dedicated wife and mother. That's my goal. Most important is that together my husband and I have provided our daughter the best upbringing we possibly can. Who knows what else may lie ahead for me, opportunity-wise or medically? But whatever it is, I'll give it my best, just like I've always done. That's the sort of person I was before my diagnosis, and that's the kind of person I'll always be. Whatever happens, I'll accept it and give it my best."

And so she has. Four years after the collapse that kept Julianne in bed for three weeks, she accomplished things that she never dreamed of. She became involved with the Muscular Dystrophy Association, giving speeches and interviews as both a spokesperson and client. She helped the MDA with their television productions, like the annual telethon fundraiser. She's active in her church and Elise's school. She's a person with unique physical limitations in her life, and she's never been busier.

To those who already know her, it's not surprising that last summer Julianne decided to try water skiing again—four years after her diagnosis. In 1993, she successfully dove off the high board in a swimming pool, so for Julianne, skiing was a natural follow-up. "Next year I want to sky dive," she said.

"Water skiing wasn't a spur-of-the-moment decision. I had thought about it a lot. Mostly, I wanted to do it for my daughter. I wanted Elise to see me try, even if I failed. I wanted to plant a seed in her that would remind her to *always* try hard at whatever she did and to never assume defeat; to use her determination and strong will in a good way. Someday later in life Elise may be told she can't do something for whatever reason. Perhaps she'll just be trying to pass a difficult test in school. Whatever the challenge, I wanted her to remember me water skiing and say to herself, 'If my mommy can, then I can too.'"

Only those people who *don't* know Julianne would have to wonder if she made it back up on water skis that sunny day in September 1993. Her daughter stared anxiously from the back of her parents' ski boat as the rest of her family cheered her on.

"It wasn't important that it took me thirty minutes to climb back into the boat. It didn't even matter whether I made it up. What matters is that I tried my best to beat the odds while planting that seed."

And by the look on Elise's face that day, Julianne planted quite a seed.

My Letter to the World

We have one world and lots of different people living in it. We all argue and fight about our differences. Just because we're different doesn't mean we have to fight or be mean. We talk about peace but never make it. We think the only way to solve our problems is to fight and that never works out.

There are so many other possibilities that would work out better than fighting. All the countries have nuclear weapons. This is dangerous and scary. When one country thinks the other country has a better bomb, then they build an even bigger one. Everyone could be killed.

I believe in a world that talks things out instead of fights it out. I believe in a world with no walls or fences so we can talk more to each other. I believe in a world with no separation.

When we go to work or school or church we should ask what we can do to make the world a better place to live in. We should all spend our money on food and stuff because then we would be too poor to build bombs.

Love,
Adrianne Richardson

*The greatest lesson of love is
found in the eyes of our children.*

About the Author

Jan Blaustone is a California native who works at home as a writer, editor, and speaker. *Every Family is Special: Love Comes First* is her second book, following her successful 1993 release, *The Joy of Parenthood* (Meadowbrook Press/Simon & Schuster).

Prior to Jan's writing career, she worked in advertising and was assistant to bestselling author, H. Jackson Brown, Jr. (*Life's Little Instruction Book*). Jan also worked as a firefighter for the Bureau of Land Management in Lake Tahoe six years prior to her diagnosis of muscular dystrophy in 1987.

In addition, Jan became a volunteer consultant in the spring of 1994 to the Muscular Dystrophy Association and a member of MDA's National Task Force on Public Awareness. She speaks nationwide on issues of interest to people with disabilities, and she is a motivational speaker to parenting groups regarding family issues. Jan donates a portion of her royalties to The National Committee to Prevent Child Abuse.

Jan currently lives in Nashville, Tennessee with her husband, Michael, a studio drummer and producer. They have one child who is three years old, two large dogs, and one fearless cat.

HEALTHY FAMILIES AMERICA

Between 1985 and 1991, child abuse reports in the United States increased an appalling 40%. And today, about 42 out of every 1,000 children in this country are reported as victims of child abuse—with the children most likely to die as a result not even five years old.

Partial proceeds of the sale of this book will be donated to The National Committee to Prevent Child Abuse and their Healthy Families America program. Because NCPCA also recognizes that "every family and every child is special," they are sponsoring this wonderful program, launched in 1992 in partnership with Ronald McDonald Children's Charities.

Healthy Families America builds on a proven, successful approach to preventing child abuse. Families are provided with intensive, comprehensive and when appropriate, long-term services for up to five years. The program begins in the hospital by providing all parents with helpful information about being a new parent. It also identifies parents who would most benefit from home visitor services.

To learn how you can help, please contact your state NCPCA chapter or call Toll-Free 1–800–55NCPCA for more information about the Healthy Families America program.

DEAR READER:

I hope you enjoyed reading this book—it's my second one. Share it with a family member, and perhaps you can drop me a postcard and let me know what you thought about it. I love getting mail, don't you? I promise to write you back.

Happy Memories,

Jan Blaustone

P.O. Box 92305
Nashville, TN 37209